CONNECTIONS

Published by WeBook Publishing – Los Angeles, CA
All rights in the English language reserved.

No portion of this book may be copied, stored in recovery systems, or transferred by any means, whether electronic or mechanical, nor photocopied, recorded, or otherwise, without the author's and the publisher's written permission.

This book is a work of non-fiction. It is based on the author's professional and personal experiences while navigating the corporate world. The opinions and methods described within this book are the author's personal findings. You may discover there are other methods and materials to accomplish the same end result.

For information, please email info@webookpublishing.com

Copyright © 2025 Adriana Alcântara
Copyright © 2025 WeBook Publishing

First English Edition

ISBN: 978-1-966892-01-4
LCCN: 2025901108
Written by Adriana Alcântara
Translators: Fernanda Alves & Nathalia Coppa
Editor: Ana Silvani
Copy Editor: Maria Acero
Cover Design: Daniel Leite Fernandes
Interior Formatting: WeBook Publishing

Manufactured in the United States of America

Note: Much care and technique were employed in editing this book. However, there can be no assurance that it will be free of minor typing errors, printing issues, or even conceptual ambivalence. In any such case, we ask that the issue be notified to our customer service at the e-mail address info@webookpublishing.com. Thank you!

ADRIANA ALCÂNTARA

Connections

The Importance of Networking and Building Relationships

WeBook Publishing - English Edition

I dedicate this book to all the women in my family who have given me their best and taught me so much.

To Vicky, the best daughter I could've asked for, and who made me the best mom I could've ever been.

To the women who continuously seek improvement in all aspects of their lives.

Acknowledgments

This book was always a huge dream that only became a reality thanks to the many people who encouraged me. I would like to thank my step-father, Attila de Souza Leão Andrade Jr. (in memoriam), who planted the seed of my becoming an author. To my special connections, wonderful women, and friends who shared their perspectives on our lessons learned. I cannot leave out friends such as Vinicius Melo, who helped me find a structure that organized what I wanted to say, Breno Lerner, Guilherme Oller, and Camila Leme—the first to read the initial version of this book and who affectionately shared their feedback. To my husband, always my biggest champion and fan, and my parents.

Thank you to Anderson Cavalcante, Diana Szylit, Nestor Turano Jr., and the whole team at Buzz Editora, who embraced this project as their own alongside me for the Portuguese edition, and to WeBook Publishing for helping it gain wings to fly the world.

Table of Contents

Acknowledgments	7
Foreword: The construction of authentic bonds	11
Introduction: The Astronaut	13
Chapter 1: Luck	17
Chapter 2: Confidence	35
Chapter 3: Courage	55
Chapter 4: Flexibility	79
Chapter 5: Emotional Intelligence	107
Chapter 6: Listening	129
Chapter 7: Empathy	163
Epilogue: About the connection we created here	175

Adriana Alcântara

FOREWORD

The construction of authentic bonds

Fabio Coelho
President of Google Brazil

As an executive of a company where the people are the greatest asset, I've witnessed the driving force that engaged teams and well-rounded leaders can execute in favor of exceptional results.

What truly distinguishes one organization from others is the quality of the relationships it nurtures, and not the quality of its processes, technologies, or strategies. Longstanding success is built on human connections—in the way we relate to one another, collaborate, and grow together. Cultivating good, strong, and genuine relationships builds confidence, engagement, and results.

It's trivial to say that technology is increasingly present in our day to day. Processes are becoming more automated and, consequently, more impersonal. What potentially hasn't become obvious is that attention to human aspects has become the main asset of companies prospering.

When all, not just managers, practice empathy, open dialogue, and the construction of authentic connections, the results emerge spontaneously. Productivity and innovation increase. The cherry on top? It creates a work environment in which people are proud to be part of and leads to the retention of talent.

In the coming pages, Adriana Alcântara presents us with stories, reflections, and personal practices that inspire us to genuinely invest in our relationships so they can evolve into generators of growth, confidence, and collaboration. Each chapter reveals that success is intimately related to one's

Connections

capacity to invest in human development and build bridges, not just between collaborators but also with their clients, partners, and society as a whole.

I conclude this preface by manifesting my desire for our connections to create workspaces where all feel valued, heard, and motivated to contribute our best.

Enjoy!

Adriana Alcântara

INTRODUCTION
The Astronaut

It was March 1974, and I wasn't due until the end of April. On a determined Sunday, my soul decided it was my day to arrive into the world. My maternal grandfather, Manoel Rezende, always happily told the story of how he arrived at the maternity ward of *Pro Matre Paulista* in São Paulo, tripping up the entrance stairs when the security guard asked: "Are you the father?" to which he proudly responded: "No, I'm the grandfather."

The ward was packed with guests waiting for the baby to be born. On the door of the room, there was an astronaut ornament, a gift from my godfather. In a time when it wasn't possible to identify the sex of the baby, each person believed what they wanted. In this case, my mother joked with my father by placing in my future crib a picture of a random newborn baby boy named Dirceu (in honor of my father), that she found in a magazine.

Everything was planned until the obstetrician, Dr. José Hammermesz, removed me from my mother's womb and said, "It's a girl!" My maternal grandmother, Zoraide Salvetti, a strong woman and entrepreneur in the 1950s, responded to my father's disappointment by saying, "Dirceu, don't be upset. She's going to be your girl forever."

I continue to be my father's forever companion, like my grandmother predicted, but in a general sense, I believe my trajectory is far from what they imagined for me at the time of my birth.

So now, the ornament on the door became a *female* astronaut. A baby girl was born. That didn't mean I couldn't go to the moon and conquer all the stars, right? I think that in 1974, my father didn't imagine I'd have an executive career while working for the most desired and respected national and international companies. I'd lead many women and many men who

Connections

always respected me. I was very, very lucky. There may have been times I was neglected for being a woman, received certain meetings "just" for being a woman, and even may have had more or less credibility for being a woman... But even still, I love being a woman! I believe that we are astronauts walking the tightrope of trying to reach for the stars and maintaining their strength in any atmosphere—or even in its absence.

When I started teaching in the graduate program at *Fundação Armando Alvares Penteado* (FAAP) in São Paulo, I was instantly nicknamed Wonder Woman—an honor, of course. However, I think every woman has her wonders, and the superpower is finding connections that allow our virtues to be spotlighted.

In the coming pages, we will discuss the power of connections for someone interested in occupying a leadership role while inspiring those they lead, how they can use these skills and strengths to achieve new heights, and the immense transformation that qualities such as courage, confidence, and flexibility can generate for business.

Following the course of my career of over thirty-years, this book tells the story of how this astronaut dreamt and conquered stars, how I empowered other women, and how I learned many things along the way (Wouldn't life be boring without new lessons ahead?). By using my journey as a backdrop, I hope to inspire you to draw your path apart from what people around you expect from you. I hope the lessons in the following chapters mark the beginning of your journey.

I was always aware of my privileges. I started working at a young age in relevant areas with many competent people around me. It's possible that, because of that, a need to prove my worthiness in each of these spaces was deeply rooted within me. Potentially, in a secret part of me that only Freud could explain.

I also don't lose sight of the privileges I've had because of my family, and the spaces I had access to. But even though I had access to these doors, many didn't open without effort. Once I made it through them, there was no doubt that I'd take advantage of the opportunity and dedicate all of myself to it. I've always liked what I did, and I wanted to do it well. What I've discovered over the years is that sometimes *just* that is enough to exceed expectations. I wanted it bad, but that wasn't all. I was also dedicated and prepared to be the type of professional that I dreamed of being and working with.

All of that being said, I feel the need to clarify that I don't consider myself the blueprint when it comes to career, motherhood, marriage, family, or anything else. But I am happy with who I've become and have plans for who I want to be tomorrow. I'm proud of the relationships I've built, the success I've achieved, and the huge fails I've endured. I hope some of the discoveries and lessons shared here can serve as tools for those who wish to be leaders one day. Everything is connected, and I believe that's how astronauts can explore other planets.

Buckle up and get ready for take off. Have a safe flight!

Adriana Alcântara

CHAPTER 1
Luck

It might be a bit strange to start a book on corporate leadership by using "luck" as the keyword. But I believe you'll agree that no other word defines my first professional job. Considering I did it when I was only a few months old.

Everything started when my mother, Leilah Salvetti Rezende, was taking me on a walk in the *Ibirapuera Park* in São Paulo and was stopped by a woman who complimented her beauty. She then asked if my mother was interested in participating in a commercial that was being produced right there in the park at that exact moment. The ad in question was for *Estrela*, the biggest toy manufacturer in Brazil, and it featured a woman pushing a baby stroller. My mother accepted right away. It's impossible to know if that compliment was genuine. As I've learned throughout my career, both in advertising and the entertainment industry, improvising is a necessity. If I were in that producer's shoes, urgently needing a baby to appear in the commercial, I would've taken the same approach. But it's a fact that my mother, blonde with blue eyes and oozing happiness as she paraded around with her first baby, probably drew some attention.

The commercial was produced by a small production company called *Diana Cinematográfica*. On that day, the ad was for a Christmas promotion called *Banquinho Estrela (Estrela Little Bank)*. It consisted of a checkbook in which each of its sixteen pages displayed the name and picture of one of the company's toys. The child would then fill out the check, sign it, and give it to an adult who'd then deliver it to Santa Claus. We could say it was an easier way to ask for a gift without wasting the poor old man's time with a letter. (Great example of an ad that worked well in the 70's in Brazil

17

Connections

but would be inadequate today. Like chocolate or sugar cigarettes, did you have those here in the States?)

As expected, my incredibly sociable mother ended up befriending the producer Arlette Siaretta. To the point where a few months after my brother Fernando was born, about four years after the *Estrela* checkbook commercial, he also starred in one of Arlette's ads. This inaugurated what came to be a huge mark in Brazil's national advertising scene: the Johnson Baby (look it up). Yes, that iconic blonde baby with bright blue eyes. He took after my mother.

I continued doing commercials for *Estrela* and other brands through *Diana Cinematográfica*. At the time, *Estrela* was the biggest advertiser in Brazil, and my Barbie commercial co-stars became household Brazilian names such as Angélica, Eliana, Samantha Dalsoglio, Adriane Galisteu... Beyond that, our house became a filming location for many shoots. Our family's home, built by my father, Dirceu Prado Alcântara e Silva, had a space for any type of commercial: pool, garden, kids room, office, cellar, walk-in closets, and beautiful bathrooms. So, any time Arlette needed a specific environment for a shoot, it was my mother she'd call. Some incredible names walked those halls, such as Brazilian actor Agildo Ribeiro, the multifaceted late-night TV host Jô Soares, the first Miss Brazil, Martha Rocha, and many more. As a child, I was always spying on the shoots thinking all of that was incredibly fun. I loved watching the behind-the-scenes and then seeing the results on TV. It was magic!

I can't say with certainty if it was my early debut in the *Estrela* commercials or if it was the years of watching them being filmed that planted the seed of what I'd end up doing with my life. Certainly, I wouldn't have imagined this could be a "career" if I hadn't been exposed to it in one way or another. However, all of this luck often distorted my view of the opportunities that came my way. On many occasions, I submitted myself to enormous volumes of work and unpleasant situations because of the pressure I felt to prove my worth. Privilege is wonderful, and we need to embrace it. However, privilege can also come accompanied by the weight of toxic expectations. It becomes a huge challenge, especially at the beginning of a career. An opportunity that came easily led me to accept difficult circumstances. And even though there were valuable lessons learned, they also hurt me immensely.

As a contractor, my father only spoke to me about careers such as medicine, law, and dentistry. I don't think he even knew about communication nor advertising. According to him, with these professions I would be autonomous, wouldn't need a boss, and would be able to control my work hours. That is a very valid point, and I made many mistakes that proved that (which I'll share throughout these pages). Ultimately, I didn't listen to my father, and I studied marketing and advertising. Years later, when I was looking for an internship in television, my mother suggested I try my luck at the production company *Casablanca*.

I'll admit this suggestion surprised me. For one, I was shocked my mother had heard about the company. Even though it was the biggest production company in the Latin American market, I figured this type of information was restricted to those in the industry. The casualness of the idea caught me off guard as well. My professors and classmates envisioned *Casablanca* as an inspiration. A production powerhouse. Apart from its size, it was the only company that had access to certain post-production technologies. It was a dream, a huge ambition to work there, and a complex goal to achieve. The competition was huge, and the access seemed impossible. I said all of this to my mother. I argued that it was unfeasible, and maybe, it wouldn't be the best way to get an internship.

"Tell them you're Adriana, Leilah's daughter from Studio 3," she insisted. "Did you not know? *Casablanca* used to be *Diana Cinematográfica*."

With this piece of information, my mother threw me for a loop. I remembered that our house was called Studio 3 because *Diana Cinematográfica* already had two other studios. If Studios 1 and 2 didn't fit the job, it would happen at Studio 3, my house.

Mrs. Leilah always empowered me to pursue the things that were important to me. When I was seven, I went to sign up for the gymnastics class at school and heard there were no more spots available. I later found out the spots were filled on a first come first serve basis. Because my classroom was the farthest from the signup area, I missed out. I didn't think this was fair, and I complained about it at home. My mother promptly said:

Connections

"If you don't agree, fight it. Talk to the school principal if needed." And I did. I went into the principal's office and stated my case. She must've thought it was strange for a tiny seven-year-old to have so many arguments. In the end, it worked out. They opened up a new gymnastics class and implemented a more just signup process.

Following what I learned at age seven, I made my way over to *Casablanca*. It was a huge house on *República do Líbano Avenue*, coincidentally across the street from *Ibirapuera Park* where all of this started. I risked it all and listened to my mother's advice. This opportunity was the result of an enormous privilege that came from my captivating mother and her ability to build relationships. All I had to do was find the courage to follow the suggestion and knock on the company's door. We can consider this the first lesson of the book: **luck without action won't get you anywhere**. We must take advantage of the opportunities that arise and transform them into concrete circumstances.

My assertion paid off as the receptionist immediately called Arlette's office, far from the most accessible person, advising them of my presence. I later discovered Arlette would enter the production company from the back so no one knew she was there, and that it was very common for her assistant to say she wasn't in when she didn't want to see anyone. This woman was pretty much an entity, and it was hard to believe someone who was barely eighteen would be able to get a meeting with her. And yet, that's exactly what happened. It took no more than ten minutes for Arlette to come to meet me at reception and to nostalgically ask about my mother, brothers, and life.

"You've grown so much! What brings you here?"

"I'm looking for an internship. I want to work in television."

Pedro Siaretta, Arlette's husband, was producing five TV shows alongside João Doria Jr., who was a partner in the recently created division of Casablanca, Broadcast. At the time, it was common for TV networks to sell slots in their programming to shows made independently. This means you'd purchase a time slot for the show, and the producer was in charge of all the publicity, not the channel. When shows lost advertisers, the risk was in the hands of the owner of the slot, not the network. Consequently, if there were lots of advertisers and commercials, the extra profit belonged to the independent producer. Within this model, Broadcast produced programs such as *Success, Business* (which later became *Show Business*), *America on Line*, and *Walking Show*, which was aired in São Paulo by *CNT Gazeta*.

"I think *Walking Show* is more up your alley. Here's what you can do: go to Pedro's office and tell him I sent you there to start working. I'll let him know you'll be there tomorrow," Arlette responded.

I already knew Mr. Pedro. He had directed me in a few commercials when I was younger. He was a charming director who struggled with remembering everyone's names, which is why he'd call everyone "child," which I saw as affectionate.

The next day, I met with Mr. Pedro on my first day of work as an "adult." I started assisting with research for the daily agendas and scripts. The following week, I sat in on a shoot for the show *Success*, in which the person being interviewed was my former Barbie commercial colleague: Angelica. She looked beautiful and had the same face as she did when I first met her. We spent the whole day filming, and later, I delivered the tape for the broadcast on the former *Manchete* TV.

I worked on every Broadcast show, but as Arlete predicted, the *Walking Show* was my favorite. It featured celebrity interviews and was generally filmed at parties, concerts, premieres, and opening nights for theatre and cinema, almost always at night. It had the youngest audience and, consequently, the one I identified with the most.

Since the agenda followed the shoot days and everything depended on the events, there wasn't a set work schedule. The only certainty was that there would be a planning meeting at 8:30 a.m. with João Doria every Monday. He was always the first to arrive, always impeccable. Whenever anyone arrived late, even just five minutes, he'd always greet them with "Good afternoon."

At the time, it was typical to arrive at work and see a "carpet" coming out of the fax machine. That pile of paper came from press agencies sending us schedules and topics that were going to happen and wanted the *Walking Show* to cover. It was during the time when the propagation of the internet wasn't even a dream, and the best way to collect information was with a phone call and notebook in hand. All research was passed on to João at the beginning of the week. As my personal preference, I advocated for the

Connections

stories relating to the arts—play openings, interviews with artists, people involved in cinema, and television...

An interesting detail about the show was that I also starred in the opening credits. When I arrived at the company, it still hadn't left its early days of production, and the crew was filming its opening scene. Mr. Pedro's idea was to have a woman holding a sign with *Walking Show* written on it, leaving only the legs and face visible as the sign would take the body's place. The host of the show was Daniela Barbieri, a beautiful woman who was very popular with the younger audience at the time. Initially, it would be she who'd play the role, but to achieve the intended results, it would be ideal to have a taller person with dance experience. Mr. Pedro suggested we hire a ballerina just for this moment, someone who'd bring the lightness and the desired silhouette.

Luck smiled at me again. If there was any ability in which I had confidence, it was my ballet skills. "I'm a ballerina," I said. Yes, going beyond being a screenwriter, I was also the body model in the show's opening credits. It was incredibly joyous seeing my dance abilities being captured on camera for posterity. It was an amazing feeling that added a deeper layer to my expectations from when I sought out that internship. While I heard many of my college classmates complaining about their jobs, saying they were wasting their potential making copies and brewing coffee, there I was. In the thick of it. Working on stories that interested me, developing and surfing the opportunities being presented to me.

How lucky, right? Being there came from the privilege of previous happenings, built around a relationship that was constructed when I was just a baby. I recognized that which is why I dedicated myself extensively to truly "deserve" the opportunity.

At which moment was the luck determined? When I was a few months old and participated in the *Estrela* commercial? Was it actually because my mother maintained a connection with the producer who ended up filming various commercials at our house? Was it this same production company becoming a legend in the market? Was it the owner of *Casablanca* having a good memory and agreeing to meet with me? Was it Mr. Pedro and Mrs. Arlette Siaretta offering me a job so easily?

Adriana Alcântara

When luck smiles at you, are you prepared to smile back?

Years later while sitting in a meeting room with my team, the situation was as follows: the cable TV channel *Cartoon Network* needed a campaign to boost the brand. However, there was no marketing budget available.

Cartoon Network has always done campaigns in Brazil to reinforce the power of the brand and its characters. Before I arrived to the channel in January of 2018, I was working at its rival channel, *Nickelodeon*. However, I must say I have always admired how *Cartoon* organized its budget to create campaigns and events and how much the brand was beloved by the public. Of course, success always brings more money, and with more money, it's easier to consistently invest and maintain the channel's visibility. Companies often lose the opportunity to stay at the top because they hold back on investments. I noticed *Cartoon Network* had that balance. It was the leading cable TV channel in audience numbers. I observed and researched their strategic moves to learn and eventually better my performance at the competitor.

In 2018, cable TV was in a very different phase than what I had experienced for many years in my career. Losing a lot of space to streaming, *Cartoon* didn't make it out unscathed from the earthquake those platforms caused. To get a sense of it, *Netflix* had already established Brazil as its second-largest subscriber base, following not too far behind the United States. *Netflix*'s Brazilian content is among the top 10 best performers within non-English language programming.[1] The growth of streaming services, in addition to the costs of cable TV, drove the segment to reach a dizzying decline.

In general, large declines tend to weaken a company's appetite for investments and budgets in different areas of a channel, including advertising campaigns. And since misfortune does not usually walk alone,

---

[1] Mariana Toledo, "Entre os conteúdos mais vistos na Netflix nos últimos seis meses, Brasil aparece entre os dez primeiros de língua não inglesa". Tela Viva, Dec 13, 2023. Available at: <https://telaviva.com.br/13/12/2023/entre-os-conteudos-mais-vistos-na-netflix-nos-ultimos-seis-meses-brasil-aparece-entre- os-dez-primeiros-de-lingua-nao-inglesa/>. Accessed on: Sept 16 2024

Connections

there was still a need to renew the character licensing. An advertising campaign would be extremely important to achieve this.

Licensing is when a company grants the use of its brand and its properties to other companies for use in the production of their products. Whenever you see a bedsheet, a backpack, a doll, with the image of Fred Flintstone, Scooby-Doo, The Powerpuff Girls, etc., it's because those companies paid for the rights to use these characters. This is one of the great assets that a channel like *Cartoon Network* can count on as revenue, as it has a vast array of characters. *Cartoon* has a production studio, and what is created there is 100% owned by the company. Consequently, businesses derived from the use of these characters are an incremental line of revenue.

At the time when our story takes place, these said contracts needed to be renewed. To arrive in good condition at the negotiating table, we needed to demonstrate each character's value. For that, we needed to "warm them up". We had to display that they had high visibility, were interesting to the public, and as a result, were interesting to companies that had the rights to use them. All of this meant that my team and I needed to find a way to set up the campaign without money.

I would consider this unlucky having arrived at the channel during that moment. But in fact, challenges of this level can motivate the search for creative solutions and continuous self-development. Perhaps the whole situation would have been resolved with a simple belief: "What has no solution, is solved." Fortunately, I was bitten by the challenge bug, and I wanted to find an alternative.

Another stroke of luck (and another piece of advice for those who desire success in life) is that I have always had incredible people working by my side. The head of marketing at *Cartoon Network* in Brazil was Renata Gasperoni. She is someone who not only gets the job done but makes everything even bigger and better. I met Renata while looking for someone from marketing for the channel. When I interviewed her, I immediately knew she was the right person to take over that role.

To add to our strong team, we had Vivi Arias. Imagine a creative person, who makes everything incredible, and connects things that didn't seem to ever connect and makes them look like soulmates. Yes, that's Vivi who I affectionately nicknamed as "Starlet." A person with unlimited

Adriana Alcântara

sparkle. With these two powerhouses, I felt as if we were The Powerpuff Girls. I knew nothing could stop us and on top of all of that, we had an incredible team supporting us.

After a lot of brainstorming, we arrived at a solution that seemed to solve all problems at once: we'd pair the *Cartoon Network* characters with an already established ad campaign in which all we'd have to do is grant the characters' images. And just like that we'd get quick and free press! However, this marriage had to happen in a way that generated significant value to the local community. Maybe because of the privilege that's always surrounded me, I'd only be comfortable utilizing something that's not mine (like an already existing campaign) if it were to generate something for the greater good and not just a corporate milestone.

Without a doubt, the best project was the *Campanha do Agasalho*, one of the most famous national welfare campaigns providing coats and blankets to those in vulnerable circumstances during the winter. In São Paulo, it's conducted by the *Fundo Social* (*Social Fund*), a government entity responsible for raising funds and general support for those in need. Putting together all these elements we had a noble cause through which value would be added to the adored brand.

It seemed like an incredible out. The channel had a pillar of content called *Cartoon Movement*, and we developed the campaign within this space that promotes diversity, accessibility, and equal opportunities, essentially helping the world. Beyond that, we could offer space within the channel's programming to publicize the campaign leading to bonus exposure from the enormous potential of audience engagement: children that engaged their families. It was the perfect plan! All that was left was getting the other side to join in.

The formula was: noble cause + impactful characters + publicizing on TV + the dream team + *Fundo Social*. At that moment, the only thing we needed to finish the equation was the last factor. For two months we called, left voicemails, sent emails...and nothing. I was extremely frustrated because we wanted to offer a platform and generationally known characters to leverage an incredibly relevant campaign to the community, and we never received a response. Rule of thumb, when a TV channel offers support, you respond because visibility is always welcome and media on TV is expensive.

Connections

With all that time gone by, I decided to take a daring step that I wasn't sure would work. I wasn't ready to throw in the towel, and I still had one final card up my sleeve that I had held onto for months. In 2019, the governor of São Paulo and the person who would ultimately have to approve that partnership was João Doria Jr., my first boss and former business partner of Arlette and Pedro Siaretta.

I called *Fundo Social* one more time, and just like months before, it went straight to voicemail. But this time, I left a different message.

"This is Adriana Alcântara, once again. I've been trying to reach you for months and haven't heard back. I figure this may be due to some distrust regarding our work so I believe it's valid to mention that I worked directly with João Doria a few years ago, and I trust he can confirm my earnestness and commitment. Today is Wednesday. Can you please get back to me by Monday morning? It's the only way our proposal can be viable. Thank you for your time."

A few hours later my cell phone rang. Who was it? *Fundo Social*. We scheduled a meeting for Friday of the same week. We arrived and there was a very strict protocol for the meeting. I had never been to a place with so many formalities and waiting rooms. It felt like we were at a meeting in the 70's. João ended up not attending, but he sent his regards and said we'd catch each other at the next opportunity. Even without his presence, the *Fundo Social* team was very excited by the proposal, very different from the impression they had given me before. We closed the partnership then and there.

The campaign was launched with characters from the shows *Ben 10* and *The Powerpuff Girls*. Beyond the costless session, *Fundo Social* secured a commercial on the *Cartoon Network* programming with our characters scattered around town on cardboard boxes. They could be found on subways, buildings, pharmacies, police stations, and every place imaginable. Even during the transmissions of rival networks. During live coverage of the *Campanha do Agasalho* on *Rede Globo*, the cameraman tried to blur the image of our characters (unsuccessfully), which appeared on the campaign boxes and posters. This attempt happened not only due to *Globo*'s policy of no indirect (and free) advertising but also because *Cartoon* was in direct competition with *Gloob*, the company's children's channel.

This occurred consistently. Anytime there was a journalistic flash of the campaign, we'd gain more visibility. My team and I had so much fun seeing the surprising places our beloved characters popped up.

That was the biggest fundraiser for the *Campanha do Agasalho* in its 71 years of existence. There were 21.8 million pieces of clothing and more than 90 thousand blankets (exceeding the projected goal of 50 thousand blankets), distributed to 1,132 entities in 221 municipalities in the state.[2] On our end, we had one of the largest advertising campaigns in the history of the channel. The investment included ten thousand dollars for the production of the commercial done in animation, which communicated the campaign, and some static artwork created by Vivi Starlet and the team, which was printed on the donation boxes, posters, and other materials. To those who found the invested amount to be high, know that it is much less than what is spent on any thirty-second animation, believe me. It even brought in spontaneous media results of two million dollars.

What was the determining factor for this to be a success story? The marketing plan we created was, in itself, bulletproof. The only obstacle seemed to be precisely the core of the government responsible for the campaign. So, no matter how perfect our project was, it could still go down the drain for the sole fact that they didn't respond to phone calls or emails. Was it divine luck to have had a professional relationship with someone who, two decades later, would become the governor?

Yes, and no.

Yes, I took a huge risk when I pulled out the governor card and got lucky. On the other hand, our project was so good that when "luck smiled at us" we were 100% ready to smile back. I believe that if it had been during any other administration than João Doria's the results would've been the same: the São Paulo government would've approved the idea. I certainly wouldn't have had a problem with contacting the governor, no matter who he was, in the same way that I went after the school's principal when I was seven to stand up for what I believe in. This project didn't just make sense

---

[2] "Campanha do Agasalho 2019 tem recorde histórico de arrecadação". Governo do Estado de São Paulo, Sept 23. 2019. Available at: <https://www.saopaulo.sp.gov. br/spnoticias/fundo-social-encerra-campanha-do-agasalho-2019-com-recorde--historico-de-arrecadacao/>. Accessed on: Sept 16 2024.

to me, but also to the community, *Cartoon* and *Turner*, the owner of the channel at the time, currently known as *Warner Bros. Discovery*.

Perhaps, in the end, what we call luck is a combination of factors. When I look at my professional life through a panoramic view, I see several dominoes being knocked down in a row. The first one being that afternoon in *Ibirapuera Park*. In a way, it is possible to reduce these incidents to luck. But even with luck, the way we act and connect the dots is essential to the result. What we call luck is actually what we choose to do when it smiles at us.

Luck is only half the battle

In retrospect, with an added maturity of fifty years, the *Walking Show* was a huge opportunity that, in a way, I didn't have the maturity to take advantage of. I was too young to assume the subsequent responsibilities, and yet, I embraced the moment anyway. This became a huge character trait of mine: eyes open and antennas tuned in for any opportunity that could arise and that I could grab. I would never say I couldn't do something, I always asked for help and learned. Because luck without action doesn't result in anything, remember?

Still, my dedication and commitment were at the expected level for a twenty-year-old girl who liked to spend time with friends, go to parties, and travel. If I had understood the size of that opportunity and the unique luck it involved, I would certainly have dedicated myself even more. I had all the financial and emotional conditions, in addition to zero pestering from my family which removed the pressure. I didn't feel an absurd need to be the best, so I could switch to a more distinguishable program at a larger network. At the same time, it was one of the jobs where I felt the most accomplished. Interviewing such different people, centered on the creative and artistic world, is electrifying. I would have easily continued to do that my whole life.

But in my twenties, I wanted to try other things, and there was still so much to study and learn. I ended up leaving *Walking Show* to work on articles for the show *Perfil*, with Otávio Mesquita. Although it wasn't my own show, it aired on *SBT*, a network with greater visibility than *TV Gazeta*. It made sense, professionally. However, the content didn't fascinate me as much, and I had no participation in story decisions. Therefore, it wasn't a happy change.

Sometimes that's how our professional journey goes, unfortunately. On the other hand, there were times when I was the right person at the right time and in the right place, and the only thing missing to align all the stars and get the happy ending was a bit of good luck and a willingness to embrace it.

But I'll tell you more about that in the next chapters...

Luck
Renata Gasperoni

When luck strikes, you need to be ready. But let's face it, to be ready, you also have to be lucky, right?

Were you born into a home that provided opportunities? Didn't need to work from a very early age to help support your family, having time and resources to study? So you were very lucky right off the bat.

Luck. Chance. Coincidence. There are many names that we attribute to this phenomenon. And my story with Adriana, author of this book, began like that.

I had been working at *Viacom* for a little over two years and had finally found a good rapport with the creative services team, largely due to the competence and professionalism of Julia Sellare, who I affectionately call Julinha. At the time, she was a part of the channel's production team and someone who became one of my dearest friends. I was over the moon! Our partnership was yielding a winning streak of projects, and we had an incredible dynamic.

One fine day, Julinha said to me: "Rê, I'm leaving. I'm going to *Turner*." Although I was very happy for her and the opportunity she had received, I was sad that our work partnership ended there.

Connections

A few months later, Julinha and Adriana, both now working at *Turner*, found themselves at the coffee cart in an empty office as they were the only ones there during a holiday.

One of the reasons Adriana was at *Turner* that day was because there was no one to lead the marketing team. The work was backlogged, and she urgently needed to hire a professional for the role. It was then that Julinha, upon hearing what Adri shared, said: "There's someone you need to meet."

That's how it went: a moment of luck that put them in the right place and right time eventually brought us together, initiating our story.

After four years of working together, the so-called bad luck decided to show up, and, on that occasion, took Adriana out of my daily life. After *Turner* became *Warner Bros.*, and soon after being acquired by the *Discovery* group, we went through a restructuring, and her position needed to be cut. It was a very fragile moment for the entire team. We weren't just losing an incredible professional who was a driving force, but a leader who contributed to the development of everyone. Someone who served as a foundation for the team.

To my great joy, after a while, our paths crossed again in the professional sphere – because we never stopped cultivating the friendship built in those years at *Cartoon Network*. Adriana was hired to lead *Audible*'s operation in Brazil and needed to assemble a local team. I was extremely honored by the invitation to participate in the selection process, and after many interviews, I was invited to lead the brand and content marketing team.

My journey thus far has taught me that luck is a collective beast. It rarely walks alone. When it smiles at people who are dear to you, it'll smile at you too. After all, more than being prepared for when luck strikes, it's the bonds we nurture that open the best doors.

Renata Gasperoni currently serves as brand and content marketing director for *Audible*. Her professional career of more than twenty years includes stints at *Warner Bros. Discovery*, as Senior Marketing Manager at *Cartoon Network*, *Viacom*, and *The Walt Disney Company*. With a bachelor's in Advertising and Publicity, Renata has accumulated experience in team management through a humanized approach and with a great focus on results.

Connecting the dots

- Luck without action results in nothing. We need to take advantage of opportunities that come our way and transform them into concrete circumstances.

- Luck puts incredible people in our path helping us build success. However, it is up to us to cultivate and strengthen these connections.

- The way we act and connect the dots is essential to transform luck into results. In the end, what we call luck is what we choose to do when it smiles at us.

Now it's your turn!

Luck is unpredictable, but we can prepare ourselves to embrace it when it knocks on our door. For this, I'd like to give you a small reflection exercise. It's a good starting point for mapping out an action plan and putting it into practice as soon as luck smiles at you. Ready?

1. List below a professional goal you'd like to accomplish in the coming months:

2. What are three things that need to happen for this goal to be reached?

3. What actions are within your reach to accomplish the items listed above?

4. What connections do you have that can help you accomplish these tasks?

SHARE YOUR ANSWERS
#CONNECTIONSBOOK

Adriana Alcântara

CHAPTER 2
Confidence

Generally, the first thing that comes to mind when using the word *confidence* in a text related to professional life is the idea of self-confidence, an almost essential characteristic when it comes to a successful career. That's not the case here. The confidence I refer to is typically known as trust. Sometimes it gets confused with security. When we are safe, it's because we have confidence in who is around us. It is this trust that we will talk about here.

This feeling is the basis for developing healthy relationships, whether familial, emotional, or professional. Personally, it is unimaginable to work in a place where there is no relationship of trust with others, especially since we spend most of the day at our job. Confidence refers to feeling comfortable getting your point across, not being in your best mood or having the same dose of patience every day, or being able to make mistakes and make things right as a team. We spend many hours with the people we work with, and I would not have the best conditions for performing well if I didn't feel safe. Trust is necessary for creativity to flow– and without creativity, there is no development. In any industry, it is the seed that causes different thoughts to be tested. Through errors, adjustments, and refinements, there is an evolution.

Over time, I realized that I was always looking for these connections. Without a shadow of a doubt, my professional achievements were only possible through the trust I had established with the people around me. I have always been very privileged in this sense.

I had been interning at the *Walking Show* for about a year when, one day, I arrived at the office and was informed that Daniela Barbieri would no longer host the show. She had recorded a commercial for a cigarette

Connections

brand, which her contract did not allow. According to the sponsors, she could not associate her brand, image, or voice with alcoholic beverages, tobacco, and similar brands. Tobacco brands generated stigma, and actors who had their image linked to one of them would be barred from working for brands that had a more traditional image. For an actor to agree to be in a commercial for a cigarette brand, the amount paid should compensate for other potential jobs that they would lose. At the time, advertising in Brazil paid very well, and this particular brand was a big customer. When I say "very well", I mean actors were buying apartments with one or two commercial paychecks, something very different from the fixed salary of a TV host. I don't know what I would have done in Daniela's place, but I do know that her decision completely changed the course of my career.

That day, we had two recordings scheduled that would set up the show for the whole week, and we didn't have a host. Complicating things a little more, we couldn't air any reruns that had Daniela. Given the legal situation, nothing, not even the ad that promoted the program, could go to air.

We needed a solution, and it was up to production to figure out what that would be. We began looking for anyone who could be the immediate replacement. We called some people–Marisa Orth, Gabriela Duarte, Carolina Ferraz, Solange Frazão–but no one had the availability to take on the project. We tried many different types of people, given the level of our desperation. But it's funny to think that if any of them had been available they could've signed on to be the new host of *Walking Show*.

"What if we have Adriana host it?" the suggestion came from Carlito Camargo, the show's director.

I admired Carlito. He studied at New York University and returned to Brazil with incredible preparation and excitement. He's the type of person who can talk about any topic and is unbelievably smart. When we'd speak he'd say I didn't seem like I was only twenty. My self-esteem would skyrocket because he thought I had something interesting to say. Carlito already had a respectable career, while I was still crawling in college.

His suggestion about me hosting the show went to Fernanda Lauer, our multi-hyphenate executive producer. The question came with certain risks. Fernanda trusts the world, everyone in it, and the universe. She always

Adriana Alcântara

looks on the bright side, is always laughing, and is willing and open. She's one of those people you trust the second you meet her. Perhaps the best way to describe her is to say that she doesn't get mad about anything. I've rarely seen her in a bad mood, and I believe she is immune to worry. Fernanda is that person who takes everyone under her wing and takes care of them as if they were her own. As soon as she heard Carlito's suggestion, she agreed.

They both called me in for a meeting, and I thought I was going to be let go. *The dream is over,* I thought. How would the show continue? What other role could they possibly offer me at the company? But I was wrong.

"What do you think about hosting the show?" asked Fê. I later found out that they had agreed that if I took more than a minute to respond, I wasn't the right person to be in front of the cameras.

In less than a second, I said, "Yes."

The two looked at each other and in a silent conversation they must have concluded that maybe things would work out after all. At that moment, we organized our action plan: I would have to go to the hairdresser to get a haircut, a blowout, and everything that was possible in the span of a few hours to make me a "presentable" host. The biggest pain point for me was the haircut. As a teenager who loved that Rapunzel-length hair, it hurt a little. So with four inches less hair and with the same clothes, I went to work that morning as a producer–a plaid wool skirt and a black turtleneck sweater–we went out with the team to record my first story. We had Ney (cameraman), Julinho (audio operator), Alemão (lights), and Edson (driver). And, of course, Fernanda, who was the boss and had more maturity than this entire group together. We looked more like children on a school trip.

The first story was recorded in the afternoon, and it was an interview with none other than Oswaldo Montenegro, whose musical *Noturno* was currently playing. I had already seen the show because a friend from my ballet days, Fernanda Safadi, was part of the cast which gave me more context on the piece. I felt so comfortable with Oswaldo that I forgot to position the microphone correctly. I improvised the first question–because that day instead of writing the script, I had to cut my hair and prepare for my new role. Talking about music, dance, and theater is what I love most, and it was too much to ask that I start my life as a host with this gift of an interview while having me pay attention to the microphone at the same time.

Connections

They even did a run-through of the show—which was an exclusive viewing for our team—to get images of it. That was the best part. It was great because the images saved my missing microphone mistakes in the final edit, while I marveled at the most amazing Tuesday I could have ever imagined.

Before leaving, Fernanda took a picture of me with Oswaldo. She had this habit: even without the ease of cellphones and digital cameras, she was crazy about photos and was responsible for documenting all my shoot days since then.

The second story was at a nightclub about the release of the Giovane vhs, the Brazilian volleyball idol, after winning the gold medal in the 1992 Olympics. Contrary to the first topic, I was never interested in sports, but I was always into the arts. I had no idea what to ask in that situation. The event was full of journalists and TV shows, but I was the newbie in the middle of that media-savvy crowd. But of course, Fernanda had an idea:

"He's hosting a press conference. We'll write down the questions, and then for the show you ask him the same questions he answered then," she said.

I think the reason behind Fernanda's idea—besides me not being a reporter and that being my television debut—was to keep me calm during the interview, as I would already know the answers. It made sense and it worked very well. Soon after, I felt very comfortable randomly approaching people and asking some very generic questions: "Do you like volleyball?" "What do you think of Giovane's career?" and so on. I never interrupted the answer because I figured that the more the interviewee spoke, the less I had to say. I didn't have the experience to hold a more fluid conversation. A lot was going on in my mind at the same time.

The recordings went to editing and dear Fernando (or Dog, as he was known at the company) was responsible for fixing all my inexperience. I sat next to him as we laughed at my lack of attention, of which there were many moments. At the same time as he was having fun, he gave me tips on what not to do. Each lesson was taught with lightness and assertiveness, which made me feel increasingly secure in the workplace. It felt like I was in a classroom, except my final project would air on a national network Saturday of that same week.

Adriana Alcântara

After the miracle performed in the editing room, I went to the studio to record the opening and closing scenes of the segments in front of a backdrop. Then it was Carlito Camargo's turn to direct me. I had been there during all of Daniela Barbieri's shoots in that same studio, and it was unbelievable that I was in her place. I remember Carlito telling me to look deep into the camera lens as if I were looking deep into the eyes of someone I loved very much.

In the studio, I didn't have to worry about the text because I was reading from a teleprompter. Older models used the famous mirror technique, reflecting the original image with the writing inverted, thus, when it was projected onto the device itself, the sentences were displayed correctly.

However, I faced other challenges. In the first takes, my eyebrows moved too much and it looked like I was grimacing. Carlito made me watch myself on the monitor to understand what was happening. I don't think anyone likes watching themselves on TV when you're inexperienced. Personally, it was a shock but very essential. We need to see mistakes to feel prepared to resolve them. There were several takes until I was able to focus on what needed to be improved. After an hour, I was on top of it. Eyebrows ready, reading from the teleprompter without any faces, and done! We got all the shots we needed in one or two takes. I don't know if I learned to read the teleprompter without making faces, or if at that point, I had already memorized the text after repeating it so much. I am immensely grateful for Carlito and the team's patience in the studio that day.

The show's completed version went to João Doria Jr. for approval. I don't know if João had the option of not liking what he watched. There were sponsorships at stake, a lawsuit between the production company and the former host, and an already purchased time slot with the network. Obviously at the time, I didn't gather all these pieces. I was just grateful for the opportunity and for the people, in whom I had a lot of confidence, supporting me. After all, that "madness" only worked because I could trust and feel safe with the team.

On Thursday, I took the tape of the recordings to TV *Gazeta*, on *Avenida Paulista*. That same day, the ads began to play during commercial breaks. My face appeared in between celebrity interviews.

Connections

The only problem was explaining all this at home. How would I tell my father that his daughter would now spend a few nights a week going to clubs to interview celebrities? Even more so since my face made me look more like I was seventeen than twenty years old–and they tried to stop me many times thinking my ID was fake. On these occasions, Fernanda had to intervene and say: "She is of age and the host of *Walking Show.*"

In a mix of nervousness and happiness, I told my family how my week had gone. My father was never a big fan of my passion for television, but he always placed great value on the act of working. It may not have been the career he envisioned for me, but he told me he was happy to see that I was evolving, learning, and taking my work seriously. In his mind, working meant having a set schedule and a rigid routine. It made sense why he didn't understand the dynamics of a TV show. But, the deal was as long as it didn't affect my grades in college, I could do whatever I thought would be worth it, with good judgment. My father trusted me, and I trusted him. That has always brought security to our relationship as a whole. We went up to the second floor of the apartment and turned on the TV to *Gazeta*. After about twenty minutes, we saw the ad together for the first time. There I was, with that same black turtleneck I wore to work on Tuesday, thinking it would be a day like any other.

When I recorded the opening credits of the show at the beginning of the internship–in which my legs appeared, with the "body" of the sign–*Veja* magazine highlighted me in *Terraço Paulistano*, a part of the magazine that shared interesting facts, under the title "The legs of Daniela Barbieri".[3] With that hook, my entry into showbiz as a host did not go unnoticed, being worthy of a note from *TV Folha* that contained two sentences. The first one was about me being the new host of the show, and the second said: "A week ago, the model–the owner of the legs that we've seen in the opening credits–replaced Daniela Barbieri."[4] My legs, which were dancing to the song "I Wanna Dance with Somebody" by Whitney Houston, now had a face and voice!

---

[3] As pernas de Daniela Barbieri. Veja, São Paulo, pp. 8-9, March 30, 1994.
[4] "Modelo apresenta 'Walking Show'". TV Folha, August 28, 1994. Available at: <https://www1.folha.uol.com.br/fsp/1994/8/28/tv_folha/1.html>. Accessed on: Sept 19, 2024.

Adriana Alcântara

The way I became a TV host so suddenly is a great example of incredible confidence on my part in accepting the challenge. This is partly true, but it wasn't because I trusted myself. It was that I trusted the people around me. I had been there less than a year, but my ideas were being heard. People cared about each other and wanted to hear each other's opinions. When we'd meet to decide what would be filmed the following week, everyone, including João Doria, asked me: "What do you think of this idea? Are you comfortable with us moving forward? Do you think this topic is relevant?"

This is incredibly important. With this type of posture, I felt valued, even when my suggestion was not accepted. We don't need to be right all the time, but we need to be heard. That allows for security in corporate environments to increase. Having an understanding of a topic or not, I had confidence in the team. I had an extremely welcoming director, a producer who was with me everywhere and took care of me, and an editor who was very attentive to the material we produced. In the end, I think my contribution was very small compared to everyone else's work. And another important point: when the most complex problems are resolved collectively and without despair, it is impossible not to have confidence and build trust.

Throughout this process, I met so many incredible people such as Julia Lemmertz, Alexandre Borges, Raul Cortez, Fúlvio Stefanini, Osmar Santos, Guilherme Arantes, Arnaldo Jabor, Leonardo Senna, Manabu Mabe, Gisele Bündchen, Serginho Groisman, Otávio Mesquita and the director of *Globo*, Roberto Talma–I ended up working with the last two in the future– and many more. Beyond our nightlife events, I had the opportunity to go paragliding, scuba diving, horseback riding, and many more adventures.

And the person who was always by my side was Fernanda, who became my older sister. She took care of me during the two years I hosted the Walking *Show*. Fernanda used to make me snacks at her own home since the show's budget was too small for that. On cold days, she never forgot to bring me a blanket, and there were many times when I slept on her lap after filming. This relationship turned into a long-lasting friendship. We had several weekend shoots so we spent a lot of time together. She'd make dinners, and I imagined that when I lived alone, my house would be like hers. There were always cookies ready to eat at any time. She always made

41

Connections

amazing food and constantly invited the whole team over for delicious dinners.

Another suggestion for confidence and trust building: I loved socializing with my team outside of work. This is not common in the corporate world, but I thought of it as natural. I felt like an adult, mature, and important. I used a pager, cell phones were not yet accessible, so production could notify me of last-minute pieces. It reaffirmed my indispensability at work. I would always reciprocate by doing my best and trusting the team with my eyes closed.

This wasn't the only time I expanded relationships beyond the work environment, and these situations can have different ways of reaching a common ground.

Confidence strengthens alongside your connections

I believe first impressions are extremely important, especially the ones I cause. Upon arriving at *Nickelodeon* as a senior production coordinator, I took over from a former professional who had left and was beloved by the team. Leading the group that remained was Luísa Fernandes. A small girl with a brave face. She knew how production worked, and all its processes, from start to finish. Her posture made everyone on the team respect her a lot.

According to Luísa herself, I have a much more vivid memory of the situation than her. From her perspective, there was initial discomfort, but the turning point didn't take long to happen. But in my emotional memory, the air of distrust I encountered seemed more like a fortified barrier with pointed stakes and barbed wire. An obstacle that I would need to overcome. It's a bit of a dramatic story, I know, but it's yet another indication of how I need to be in an environment of trust between all parties– at the very least, among those under my leadership.

Once this discomfort passed it became obvious that we would become great friends. We are very similar in the way we work. A very Cartesian and serious way of dealing with daily problems, despite the twenty-odd years of experience. We were young women who needed to prove themselves at every moment in the corporate world, who took advantage of every opportunity along the way and who believed in the work. So, we did our best. We were extremely methodical, organized, committed, and perfectionist. Moments of relaxation need to exist, but the professional worker must be taken seriously.

This is a recipe for disaster and leads to the normalization of unacceptable circumstances. Not that the other people on the team, also very young, didn't have professionalism, but I feel that the commitment that we both had to do our jobs brought us closer. There were almost no limits to what we were willing to execute to not drop the ball. We came together at work and in our personal lives, always supporting each other. We started seeing each other on the weekends. We'd spend so much time working that we ended up talking about what we were going to do on our days off and we soon ended up merging our calendars. We bought theater tickets and arranged lunches and dinners. Knowing how to separate your personal and professional lives while also enjoying the best of both is key to building connections in the corporate world. Luísa and I met each other's families, we opened our hearts and shared personal problems, and although we worked long hours, we found time to have fun.

The fact that we had a difficult boss also strengthened our connection because we needed to work around real challenges and ones inflicted by him. Together we were stronger, and with that, our bond of confidence also grew stronger every day. When I say "a difficult boss", I'm talking about a person with an extremely volatile mood. One day everything was well, and the next, everything became a problem. In this scenario, we were constantly tense while not knowing what the workday would be like, as it depended on a state of mind unrelated to corporate deliveries and results. Often, the volume of hours worked was not acceptable, the tone of voice was not appropriate, nor was the way we were treated. We didn't know it, or rather, we simply didn't contest it. In my case, I think the constant privileges I had experienced normalized everything that happened.

One of our classic stories was when I had to lock up a FedEx delivery man in a room. Yes, you read that correctly. I confess to executing false imprisonment.

To understand this story, it is necessary to understand the context in which everything happened. In the early 2000s, the transmission process

Connections

of our programs happened as follows: all filming was recorded on tapes that, after being edited, were sent once a week via FedEx to the United States. In the same style as the tape for *Walking Show*, but the *Nickelodeon* one needed to cross the hemisphere and go to the office in Miami, where our headmaster would watch the show. Another tape headed to New York, which was responsible for the satellite transmission of the programs. It was a process without much margin for error. If we couldn't get that tape in the mail on the exact day, there would be no show to air.

Believe it or not, this had already happened because of hurricanes in the United States and the Caribbean that prevented the arrival of the plane with the tapes. In these situations, the channel would air reruns. But even in this unpredictability of extreme natural events, when everyone was aware of the event, it generated a lot of complaints from advertisers and the audience. Now, when the fault was human and taking into account the boss we had...Well, let's just say it was a situation that we didn't want to experience.

The second piece of context is that once a year we hold the *My Nick Awards* event. In the United States, this award is called the Kids' Choice Awards, where children choose the winners in several categories, such as best animated show, best actor, best band–everything from a child's perspective. It was like the Oscars for children. The awards were given out at a big event, which was pre-recorded and then aired during the week of Children's Day, which is celebrated in October in Brazil. This event brought in a high percentage of revenue from advertisers, and therefore the pressure to deliver high-quality results was very strong, as the intention was always to renew sponsorships and to bring in more supporters. The show was typically staged at Playcenter or Hopi Hari, popular theme parks in Brazil. On the day of the event, the parks would close and only be available for guests of the channel and sponsors.

It was an event that we spent the entire year organizing, in parallel with our typical programming. To get an idea of the scope, we spent about two weeks working extremely late nights editing and polishing all the content that would air on TV, when typically a traditional show takes about six hours to edit.

On the last day, when we were making copies of the beta tapes that were going to be sent to the United States, we had a problem.

Adriana Alcântara

The programs were edited in low resolution so as not to compromise the memory limitation and speed of the equipment. After the show was edited, only the parts used in the final cut were exported into high resolution, to be finalized to go to air. At the time, the logistics were all manual. The recording tapes were kept under lock and key until the show went to FedEx and we were certain we wouldn't need them anymore. Then they are released for reuse in another recording. Everything is very different from the technology we have today.

I don't know what happened that day, but one of the tapes was recycled and erased before the program was switched to high resolution. Without the recording tape, we would have to remove the used segments in that edited version and replace them with parts of the tapes that we still had saved. This process would consume extra time that we did not have. It was then that reception called us saying that the FedEx employee had arrived, but the program was not ready to be sent–we were still in the process of copying a recording of an hour and a half, and unlike what happens in our digital age, this is not something that happens quickly. The first solution was to buy some time. We asked him to wait a bit, as we were "almost" finished. He didn't like the idea very much, as he also had a schedule to keep. The second solution was a little more…drastic.

"Luísa, here's what we're going to do: you stay in the editing room and work on that, I'm going to offer the FedEx guy a coffee and lock him in the production room," I said. I don't remember very well what she answered, but I'm pretty sure it was something along the lines of "You're crazy" and "We're going to get arrested."

Should I have begged the delivery man for a bit more time so we could finish solving the problem? Yes, I did that, but it didn't work.

Could I have accepted our fate and then explained to our higher-ups that the biggest event of the channel, which we spent the entire year organizing to be televised around the world, would not be transmitted due to a technical issue and that we didn't have any blame in the situation?

I could, but I knew it wouldn't work.

"It's the only way," I decreed.

And that's what we did: the guy went in for a coffee and, without realizing it, was locked in the room. In my memory, it was no more than five

Connections

minutes, but I'm sure it lasted longer. When we finally finished we didn't even check the mastering, as we ran the risk of the delivery man refusing to hand over the tape if it took us even longer to free him. (In fact, that's exactly what he said when we opened the door and he came out of the room seething with rage. Maybe it was the despair on our faces that convinced him otherwise.)

Looking back today, what I did was disrespectful towards the delivery man, who had no fault and who certainly had more tasks to do. But in the scenario we found ourselves in, it was the only viable solution. We never saw him again, but I want to have it on the record here our deepest thanks and sincerest apologies for the inconvenience.

Confidence

Luísa Fernandes

It was early 2002, I had been an assistant director at *Nickelodeon* for about a year when Drica arrived to coordinate the team. We were really young and the connection was not immediate.

We came from very different worlds and backgrounds. Drica already had rather robust baggage for her 27 years. Whereas I, at 23, still crawled.

I can't say for sure when this connection was initiated, but the fact is that she became a very strong professional inspiration.

We had an intense shooting routine, we spent ten to twelve hours together per day, and Drica was always very generous, a team partner, and wise with resolutions.

In just a few months, we had already formed a strong bond of trust and friendship. We got so close that eight months later I got married and she was my maid of honor!

We have many stories from that time like the FedEx one, which Drica shared earlier and the numerous long nights in the editing room. Between one render and another (the point in which the raw material gets passed to high resolution and we don't have much left to do other than wait for the process to finish), she'd put two uncomfortably hard chairs together, and there she'd fall asleep, and I would ask myself: "Who can sleep in these conditions?!"

Adaptability is one of her most distinct characteristics. Adapting to what the circumstances offer and extracting the best from them. There are so many incredible stories from that time, but we also had terrible episodes. In times when there were no open discussions on harassment or safety at work, we were victims of dozens of abusive episodes. Despite the setbacks, we walked hand in hand accepting a lot of things we didn't know what to call and were only able to process later.

Our professional and personal lives continued to intertwine. In 2006, I had my first daughter, Nina, who also became Drica's goddaughter.

We worked together on other occasions, and I always learned a lot from her. I was constantly encouraged to do my best and to be aware of my potential and development.

For over ten years, we've followed different professional paths without ever losing sight of each other, even though we have lived in different cities for more than half a decade. This is largely due to the collecting power Drica has and the ability to maintain ties. In 2011, we had daughters practically at the same time, and since they were babies, Clara and Vicky also became best friends.

Drica built a solid executive career, traveled the world, and is always motivated by challenges. She does this with endless humility and generosity, so wherever she goes, she creates connections that last.

At fifty years old, I see Drica as a sunflower who always grows toward the light, seeking the best in herself and others. I think it is in this light that we find ourselves.

Connections

> **Luísa Fernandes** is the mother of Nina, Clara, and Chico (a beloved pet), and Renato's companion for over twenty years. Cancerian at heart, lives in São Paulo, passionate about literature, good food, and encounters with friends as well as being addicted to podcasts and good coffee. In the entertainment industry, she found her professional passion, and as an artistic director, specializing in educational content and live broadcasts, is always on the move and in constant learning.

A safety net built with many hands

The main point of confidence is the safety net we create in a team. This ultimately provides a more comfortable base for you to take risks, innovate, and make mistakes because you will have the protection of your trusty relationships.

I don't think there's a magic formula for creating these bonds that help us climb the corporate ladder, but some ingredients help a lot. Transparency, synergy, and empathy always provide good results.

Transparency means showing that you, even as a leader, don't know everything, and your team may know more than you on many subjects. After all, we are the result of a repertoire that is unique to each of us, of the situations we live through, our families, and our interests. It's always worth it to listen to others. It's also an opportunity to show our vulnerability. Being transparent when we don't know the answer and when we make mistakes is very powerful. Allowing others to help, even if you are the boss, can be transformative.

Synergy occurs when, thanks to transparency, we find common ground in thoughts, ways of being, and working—essential for continuing to grow healthily as a team.

Empathy is the ability to put yourself in someone else's shoes. The starting point is to understand that they're human and that there is a lot of context surrounding that person. Being open to hearing that they're not okay, and for example, having a family concern brings the professional and the personal together. This allows us, leaders, to be more comfortable sharing when it is our turn to not be having the best of days. After all, we all have good and not-so-good moments, and it is only through this empathetic process that we strengthen our connections.

I was fortunate to meet many inspiring human beings along the way who were open to welcoming me or being part of my team. Like a dance, I managed to get the steps right with many people who, for the most part, remain connected to my personal and professional story.

Today, as I write this book, I have the privilege of having an admirable woman as my boss, who I trusted since my first interview for the position I hold, general director of *Audible* in Brazil: Susan Jurevics. In these almost two years together, Susan has demonstrated great confidence in me.

Unlike the two examples I shared previously with Luísa and Fernanda, where we built our bond of trust over time, with Susan, it was immediate. Maybe it's because we both have more maturity, perhaps it's because we are similar—and I love to think that we are because I see her as an example. Maybe there's no explanation. I would like just to reinforce that, in one way or another, people can only perform their best when they trust others and feel that others trust them.

Confidence

Susan Jurevics

One of the things I like so much about my 50s is being comfortable in my own skin, and having confidence in myself, my expertise, my judgment, and my decision-making capabilities. Central to all of these traits in both business and in life–confidence, acumen, wisdom, understanding, listening to my instincts–is trust.

In my own experience, finding ways to quickly and genuinely build trust in teams and in companies to deliver outstanding results is one of the most important acts of a leader. Yet, true leadership begins not when others trust you, but when you trust yourself. There is a well-worn phrase, "Good judgment comes from experience, and experience comes from bad judgment." Accepting and owning your errors, learning from mistakes and regularly seeking constructive feedback–even when it stings–allows you to be vulnerable and human. It's a signal to others that continuous learning and curiosity are important.

This is true when individuals report to you directly, and even more so when they don't–and you have to lead through influence. Finding meaningful common ground beyond superficial aspects means you have to first be willing to ask probing questions and to actively listen to their answers. It's about creating the psychological safety for everyone to be able to be their own selves and do great work without negative judgment. It's about being willing to explore different perspectives and points of view to enrich results.

I started at Audible in 2019, after a long career in entertainment and media in the US and UK. Nine months later, we were sent home due to COVID-19. I started running our international business in June 2020. Seemingly overnight, I went from commuting into the office and getting to know my colleagues in meetings and happy hours to seeing numerous, unfamiliar faces in small squares on screens at what felt like all hours of the day and night. It would be more than 18 months before I'd be able to meet my team in person in their home cities–London, Berlin, Sydney, Tokyo and others. Invariably people would say, "You're taller than I thought." It became critical during these days to find common ground that would help my relationship-building with this team. Luckily, I had lived and gone to school in both London and Sydney, and had spent nearly 15 years working for Sony and Shiseido–prestigious Japanese companies–while working in global marketing and business roles that took me all over the world. My experience gave me much-needed credibility with a skeptical audience.

The difficulties of hiring in this environment became evident, quickly. My typically tried-and-true method of having a meal with a candidate before making an offer to ensure we fit was nearly impossible: we were in the midst of a global pandemic, in a high-growth category, with content consumption exploding. We needed to rely on piercing questions in a limited number of conversations to swiftly assess skills and cultural fit.

Adriana Alcântara

The labor market was tight, and it seemed that talented leaders had multiple options.

It was under these conditions that Adriana and I first met in November 2021. Audible had identified Brazil years ago as a target for a dedicated audio service, and I was looking for a leader to build and manage our business there. I felt disadvantaged from the start–I had never been to Brazil, I didn't speak Portuguese, I had no professional or personal connections in the country, and Audible had had a series of false starts that led to doubtful partners and media. Though, Adriana and I had been educated at the same school (NYU), and she had worked for American companies in senior marketing and business roles. Meeting her solely through video and finding common ground in our academic and professional experiences convinced me she was a strong fit for the role.

Flying to São Paulo in May 2022, I greeted Adriana on her first day at Audible and begin the lengthy and complex process of establishing the spoken word category and setting up our business in Brazil. From the start, we each had faith in our own and each other's judgment and a shared goal of presenting an incredible service to Brazilian listeners. Adriana had many important connections in the country. I had the knowledge of how things worked at Audible. Over the next year and a half, we each experienced personal and professional challenges that required us to pivot our plans, adjust our ambitions, and recraft what could be realistically delivered. We talked constantly through video, texts, and emails, getting to know each other and exploring possibilities for this fledgling business we both believed in. Trust was a key input that made it possible for us to realize our own capacity and resiliency.

On October 3, 2023–as I've said, one of the best days of my professional career–Adriana and I, and our small local team delivered a delightful service to Brazilian listeners. With the support of our CEO, parent company *Amazon*, content partners and a dedicated team in the US, we hosted a phenomenal press conference and celebratory publisher party in Sao Paulo, with a simultaneous Brazilian-themed party at *Audible* headquarters in Newark, New Jersey. The photo of Adriana and I hugging after the press conference, crying, said it all. This photo proudly hangs in my home office, next to a post-it note that says, "You can do hard things." I

Connections

believe that the trust we had in each other, and in our shared mission, made this possible.

This experience underscored for me the importance of trust and of empowering others as a result of my presence. My primary job as a leader is to create the conditions for my team–Adriana–to fully realize their own capability and power.

> **Susan Jurevics** joined *Audible* as vice president and general manager in 2019, became responsible for the international area in 2020, and international brand director in 2022. In this role, she is responsible for *Audible*'s business in a global scope and leads brand management, brand and content marketing, creative and social. She is a veteran media and consumer brand executive with over twenty years of experience at leading brands such as *Pottermore*, *Sony*, *Shiseido*, and *Nickelodeon*. Most recently, Susan served as global president of *BareMinerals* for *Shiseido*. Before this role, Susan worked in London as CEO of *Pottermore* by J.K. Rowling. She held various positions at *Sony* throughout her thirteen years and was a pioneer within the function of entertainment marketing between companies of the group. Susan has an MBA from NYU Stern and the Australian Graduate School of Management, and a degree in visual arts from the College of the Holy Cross and the University of London. Susan serves on the NYU Alumni Association Board, NYU Stern Executive Board, and Brooklyn-based BRIC Arts & Media, and is a creative judge at FWA, a daily digital award. She and her family reside in Brooklyn, New York.

Adriana Alcântara

Connecting the dots

- Confidence means feeling comfortable in sharing your point of view, talents, and vulnerabilities while allowing yourself to make mistakes with those who walk alongside you.

- Having confidence is a foundational block for being creative, which is fundamental for development. Creativity is the seed that allows for different thoughts to be tested, which through trial, error, and refinement generate an evolution.

- One way or another, people can only perform at their best when they trust others and feel as if they're trusted.

- Confidence is built with many hands. It is a safety net that supports us when it's time to step out of our comfort zones and take a risk, innovate, make mistakes, and adjust throughout our professional journeys.

SHARE
YOUR ANSWERS
#CONNECTIONSBOOK

Connections

Now it's your turn!

As you can see, confidence and trust are essential for us to develop. And, despite it being built by several hands, it is always important for us to reflect on our connections, assessing whether we need to strengthen some bonds in our safety net. Use the space below to map what you do to build safe environments and what actions you can take in your current relationships to create more confidence and trust.

CHAPTER 3
Courage

In the same way, positive things we are not ready for can happen to us, some things need to go wrong before they work out. Something along the lines of "everything happens at the right time." And while we wait for this time to come, we need courage to continue following our path or have courage to adjust our route when necessary. Perhaps this is one of the most important lessons that I have tattooed in my mind, but paradoxically, I still insist on not learning. It's as if our brain isn't doing the right thing, even though it knows the difference between right and wrong.

Calm down. Let's start from the beginning, two and a half decades ago.

The courage to pursue your dreams

When I started hosting the *Walking Show*, I joined a group of hosts who covered events with celebrities and famous people. We always ended up seeing each other at the same events and parties to cover the same stories. (A huge lack of creativity, as there is no shortage of entertainment in São Paulo, but that was what happened.) Otávio Mesquita with *Perfil* broadcast early mornings on *SBT*, Amaury Jr. with *Flash* on Band, journalist Goulart de Andrade with his *Comando da Madrugada*, which at the time was on *Rede Manchete*, and Celso Russomanno with *Circuito Night and Day* on *TV Gazeta*.

As you can see, the fish out of water in this group was me. Not only was I the only woman but also the only person in their early twenties.

Connections

Luckily, I was very well welcomed. I think my reality was so different from the ones they were used to–everyone did this type of work and already knew each other for many years–in the end, they enjoyed talking to me just because I had different things to say, a perspective outside their age range. My participation alternated between talking about new topics, talking about myself, and being treated like the newcomer mascot that everyone wanted to care for and welcome. I conducted countless interviews with people from the arts, cinema, television, sport, music, and many other areas because I was introduced by one of these dear colleagues through a simple and affectionate: "Hi. Have you met Adriana Alcântara, from the Walking Show?"

When Russomanno decided to run for federal deputy by giving up his career in media, Drica Lopez replaced him and kept me company in what used to be The Boys Club. Because she was older, Drica and I only had our names in common. She already had a career as a model and brought more baggage in that sense, so the mascot role continued to be mine. In the inevitable encounters during the events, we spent much time chatting and laughing, while our teams prepared the cameras and lights. We talked about everything: interview tips, upcoming story ideas, and travel tips (which were often not within the reality of my salary or interest of my age group, but I listened carefully). Much of what they said added to my development, and here's another lesson: always be open to listening to different things because there will be hidden treasures in each word.

Come to think of it, I always liked talking to all kinds of people. When I was about eight years old I was at the *Hotel Casagrande* in Guarujá, and my father left me at the pool and went for a walk. There was only an elderly man at the pool, and my stepmother mentioned to my father that I wouldn't be able to make friends. Half an hour later when they returned, the man was competing with me on who could hold their breath the longest below water! In short: I'm a talker, so it doesn't matter who it's with or what topic.

Returning to the host nonsense, in a demonstration of how there was lots of collaboration in our line of work, instead of seeing each other through a competitive lens, during shoots we'd often interview each other. It was a lot of fun. We'd always let each other know when the show was going to air, so everyone could watch the final version. Otávio Mesquita was the first person who interviewed me in my life in that very moment. He asked me how I had become the host of the *Walking Show*, already knowing that it all started with my legs. He also came to the interview very well-informed about my career and the commercials I'd done as a child–TV production professionals move a lot between broadcasting and production companies and end up exchanging valuable information. That was one thing that caught my attention: how these shows covered so many different topics. This group knew everything! They'd read about events, politics, entertainment, opportunities, trends. Always staying up to date. In the early days of the internet and without Google in our lives, staying informed was a time-consuming task and required dedication. It wasn't as easy as it is nowadays, but they could handle it.

From this experience, I received an invitation to become a host on *Perfil*. Since the show was daily, the work schedule was getting difficult for Otávio Mesquita to accommodate–and he couldn't be in two places at once. It also made sense that some of the topics that the show wanted to cover were presented by a woman. And of course, these topics included the world of aesthetics, beauty, and cuisine. Themes that were commonly associated with something exclusively feminine at the time.

Although these weren't exactly my biggest areas of interest and expertise, this was an opportunity for me to move to a bigger network, SBT, and to a program with a larger audience. Of course, I accepted the challenge! In addition to hosting, I also acted as the "youth" story consultant for *Perfil* by supporting the director Andrea Setti, the boss of everything. Years later in 2014, Andrea and I worked together again with her being the director of the main show on the *Food Network* channel, for which I was responsible for marketing, local production, and digital strategies. But that's a story for another time.

It was in this context that the idea for Otávio to set up a video social column, and I suggested Luciano Huck's name for the host of the skit. Luciano would only film the opening on camera and then narrate the events over images of the São Paulo nightlife. *Perfil* had sponsors who used to circulate in the high society, so the idea was to look for someone who fits in with this audience, who could help attract more investors, and who was

Connections

young–that is, someone who nowadays would be classified as an "influencer." Luciano already had a social column in *Jornal da Tarde* and he also did voiceover work on *Jovem Pan*. However, the main attraction was that, at the time, he was one of the partners at *Bar Cabral*, a hotspot for the wealthy young adults of São Paulo. A place where I ended up filming sometimes with the shows I hosted and also attended regularly with my friends. Luciano was there every day and had a close relationship with the regulars and with potential new sponsors. Friendly and charismatic, his debut on television was with us and it worked–really well! From there, Luciano went to *CNT/Gazeta*, with a show based on *Circulando*, his social column in *Jornal da Tarde*. A while later he blew up with *Programa H*, on *Band*, and later went to *Rede Globo*, where he is to this day. He grew as a host through his effort, charisma, and dedication. I admire his career and the way he contributes to helping people and making the world a better place.

At that time, information about the entertainment industry came exclusively from the print media, and I had the habit of reading the TV section of the newspaper *O Estado de S. Paulo*. On a Sunday morning, I came across the note that the legendary Roberto Talma–who I had the chance to interview when I was on the *Walking Show*–director and producer of several classic Brazilian television dramas, was leaving *Rede Globo* to produce soap operas in São Paulo. That was already good news to me because Talma's soap operas, being on *Globo*, were always in Rio and impossible to participate in any way. Now he planned on making his soap opera independently, through the production company JPO, in partnership with João Paulo Vallone. Dramaturgy has always fascinated me, and the desire to be an assistant to a director like Talma was a constant thought.

After I started working in television and understood better that much of the success of a television product is due to the work of producers, I started to follow some of these behind-the-scenes magicians more closely–and Talma was the one that I admired the most. He had done practically everything: he was a dancer, an actor, and even attained the role of general director, but it was his most recent work that demonstrated his capacity as a visionary.

In the mid-1990s, the country's main network, *Rede Globo*, seemed to have forgotten an important segment of entertainment, which was preteens. There was a hole between the productions that focused on children and something closer to the "six-o'-clock soap operas", which were lighter stories, sugar-coated romances with a comedic tone, and without explicit violence or spicy scenes, but it still did not speak to the young adult audience. Considering that in the 1990s, open television was still the largest source of entertainment and information in the country, maintaining young people's connection with television until adulthood was a strategic matter.

At that moment, the closest thing that was on Brazilian television for this audience was the show *Confissões de Adolescente* (*Confessions of a Teenager*), from *Cultura* TV. The success was great, and even the timid strength of *Cultura*'s TV audience was enough to bother *Globo*, who ended up taking the star of the show to their network: Deborah Secco, only twelve years old at the time.

In the following season, the chemistry between the new cast was not the same. I must share that I participated in the auditions to be the replacement, but I was too unprepared as an actress and older than Daniele Valente. So, even with a face that hid my age, I wouldn't believably play her younger sister. Despite the undeniable success, the show did not yet have the impact that a similar work would have on a channel with *Globo*'s audience.

Talma shared, years later, that he discovered this niche and realized how it was unintentionally underutilized. In the end, his instinct proved so correct that *Malhação* became a source of new talent in all areas of television dramas–direction, production, script, and of course, acting–in addition to remaining on the air for more than two decades uninterruptedly. At that time, the show was just the new hit of the moment, and perhaps not even Talma himself had any idea of the resounding success that *Malhação* would become. Coincidentally, he left *Globo* precisely to produce a soap opera that would seek to rival one of his greatest creations. It was *Colégio Brasil* and would air on *SBT*.

The story was a mix of *Dead Poets Society* with a cool teacher seeking to raise his students to their fullest potential within a conservative school structure, with the addition of swoony romance where the beautiful teacher catches herself in a love triangle between the handsome boyfriend

Connections

and the school's gym teacher, played by Afonso Nigro, and the charming but disruptive new literature professor, played by Giuseppe Oristanio.

Once again, I don't know if the world is too small or if opportunities revolve energetically in the same spaces, but the actress selected to play the teacher in the soap opera was Patrícia de Sabrit, who a few months earlier had replaced me on the *Walking Show*. Sometime later, she would nominate me to replace her as the protagonist in a children's play, due to her schedule: *A Pedra Mágica*. It was when I had the opportunity to spend more than a year on stage in the main room of the Ruth Escobar Theater, in Bela Vista, São Paulo. Since then, this has been another long-lasting friendship I've built.

When I read that the *Colégio Brasil* shoots would take place in São Paulo, I decided that I needed to work on this project somehow. Since the main location of the story is a school, they needed many people to form an entire class of students. So, I decided that my best chance would be to get a role as a student, but I was already a little older than many of the actresses auditioning. Patrícia herself, who would play the teacher, was a year younger than me, but this time my baby face, which often harmed me, worked in my favor. I went to JPO which, according to the Yellow Pages–those monstrous books with more than a thousand pages once used to search for information– was in the neighborhood of *Moema*, in the south of São Paulo.

I arrived there with a clean face and all my courage. I said to Talma: "I want to work on this soap opera with you."

I've always wanted to explore all sides of television. I didn't want to be the one who only knew how to write, host, or direct and edit: I wanted to know everything!

He opened the camera to film and asked me why.

"Because I admire your work so much," I replied. I couldn't have been more direct. "I believe I have much to learn from you, and I want to learn to direct. So, if you hire me as an actress, you'll get an assistant intern when I'm not filming. Another pro for you is that since I am of legal age, you'll have one less set of parents driving the production team crazy."

He burst into laughter. Because I did so many commercials as a child, I knew very well the dynamics of a minor on a set.

"You must have more production experience than a lot of people have work experience", he replied.

And I got it! It was a small role, but it was mine. Since my intention was simply to be there to see Talma work, this was a huge achievement for me. Even on days when I didn't need to be there because we wouldn't be shooting any of my scenes, I would go to set to watch Talma's work. This involved me standing next to him in the editing room.

Here is a brief explanation: a soap opera's programming is daily, so there is little time between recording and editing an episode before it airs. Everything is done during the pre-cut, while the scene is being recorded, which reduces editing work and helps the soap opera release one chapter per day. At the time of the pre-cut, only the director and the editor (and, in this case, me!) are in the editing room. In works like this, you need to be a very skilled director, as three to four independent cameras are filming several takes, and the pre-cut happens immediately.

Talma was very caring and welcoming, but when he got angry, it was best to get out of the way. He said interesting things, to which I paid attention. On the other hand, there would occasionally be some inappropriate things said, some dirty jokes... Once again, I was in an all-male environment and needed to deal with that. Over time, I became invisible, and they spoke as if I wasn't there.

At one point, he mentioned that he needed to find a classical ballerina for a scene with a boy in a wheelchair dreaming of meeting his mother, who was a ballerina. It would be a playful scene on the school playground, and in it, the boy would be able to walk. Promptly, I raised my hand.

I didn't even ask if there would be any payment. I have always dedicated myself regardless of how much I would receive for a job. I trusted the universe that the return would come at some point whether it be financially, experience, or connections. I believe that there are several ways for recognition to arrive, and if we are too short-sighted, we end up burning out possibilities and risk missing out on opportunities. I was no longer the ballerina I had once been, and I could certainly find someone sharper who would earn compensation, but since I didn't say anything, I arrived happy and content while transforming myself into the ballerina they needed,

Connections

wearing my clothes and ballet slippers. In other words, I didn't give any unnecessary work to neither the casting department or the costume designer. That recording resulted in one of the most beautiful professional photos I have as an actress.

This collaboration with Talma–who always had a lot of patience with me since he saw my genuine interest in everything, creating an informal relationship of master and apprentice lasting nine months for the duration of the soap opera. It was never explained why but from one moment to the next it was defined that the show would end–at least I for one never knew why it all ended so abruptly. The fact is that, from the day the decision was made onwards, the whole story had to be resolved in three episodes. *Only in television...*

Coincidentally, at that same moment, I was completing my degree. It was June 1995. Sometime before I had already started harboring the idea of getting a master's degree from New York University (NYU)–an idea planted in me by Carlito from the *Walking Show*–which began in January of the following year. So, I asked Talma if he thought that would add value to my CV.

"For sure! If you have the opportunity, you have to take it," he said. And if there was a voice of wisdom I was listening to at the time, it was Roberto Talma's. I took a deep breath and went, even though I was scared and insecure. I felt that this experience would open doors for me.

As he suggested, I started dreaming about living in New York and studying at one of the most prestigious universities. I finished FAAP in mid-1996, and the course at NYU would begin in early 1997. The diploma hadn't even gone to print when I moved to Miami in an almost impossible mission: getting a good grade on the Graduate Management Admission (GMAT) and Graduate Records Examinations (GRE) to be accepted into the course, despite my average English.

For four months, I studied hard and still needed to familiarize myself with a laptop as the exams would be taken digitally and not on paper. At that time, I had never had a computer at home. I hadn't taken a computer course, so in addition to discovering and learning the content and deciphering the language, I had to juggle the technology.

Adriana Alcântara

It was a tough challenge with time being short and having yet to perfect my English. So much so that I kept moving forward but always with a suspicion that it wouldn't work. What kept me going? My courage. To learn vocabulary, I covered my Miami apartment with cards, on which I wrote the words and their meaning to be able to memorize them. They were on the fridge, bathroom mirrors, bedroom, living room, anywhere I could put them. I studied ten hours a day, seven days a week. But I felt supported when I heard my father say that I had to have the courage to chase that dream.

The day of the exam arrived, and it would be done by computer, in a school reserved for this. My father dropped me off and said, "Good luck, give it your all." And I did. Time was short for questions, but I felt ready for the challenge. As I saw my evolution during the preparation I became more and more motivated and this brought even more energy. I took a deep breath, I don't remember if I prayed for anything, but I certainly thought about that, from that moment on, the responsibility left my hands and was up to destiny. And then, I pressed the "submit" button.

My grade wasn't astronomical, but it wasn't bad, and I knew that I had a chance if I submitted a good application to NYU. Despite being much younger than the average person applying for a master's degree at the time, I had lots of experience for my age.

I did my best and sent the letters of recommendation–including that of a former student of the university and mentor, Carlito Camargo, and director of FAAP, Rubens Fernandes–who would later invite me to teach at the college. And so, I waited. A month later, I was in New York to spend a weekend with a friend and I went to the university campus to see if there was any answer. There wasn't. A bit of despair kicked in. A whole month and nothing? There should have been some answer since classes would start soon.

Despite my nervousness and fear, everything was out of my control. There was no point in thinking about it. When I returned to Miami, I found a letter in the mail from NYU.

You know those movie scenes when a young person has been waiting for their university acceptance letter for months? When the letter finally arrives, there is that tense moment in which the envelope is opened, the fear of the words that that piece of paper contains is so overwhelming

Connections

that many ask someone else to read it. Well, it's all real. I had to read it myself, and I burst into tears with so much joy.

Years later, back in Rio de Janeiro, Talma was working on a project in partnership with Rafael, his son, and he requested a meeting to show this project to Oi TV's head of content. At that time, I had changed my field and was venturing into the challenge of launching a subscription TV service at a telecommunications company. Surrounded by men, mostly engineers, I was happy to welcome Talma to see the project.

"I don't know if you remember me...," I started, as soon as I looked at him.

"You are very familiar, but..."

"*Colégio Brasil*," was all I said.

He burst out laughing and remembered the many hours he spent with me in the editing room. He said:

"Our beautiful ballerina!"

We never know which part of a job will make an impression on people. We don't even know what will become of the work itself. Often, it is the courage we demonstrate in certain situations. Sometimes you need to find the courage to raise your hand and say: "I'll do it, leave it to me." It's what they always say about leaving your comfort zone: it may give you butterflies, but that's where the magic is, right on the other side. You just need to have the courage to reach it.

In the end, the nostalgic conversation ended there. Maybe I should have said how much I learned from him, and how his encouragement was essential for me to go to New York. Or maybe he was tired of hearing how much he contributed to someone's career. Just take *Malhação* as an example–everyone in the first few seasons of the soap opera owes their careers to him, and indirectly, everyone who came after. Maybe nothing needed to be said. After all, there he was making his pitch to the young woman who wouldn't leave him alone almost two decades ago. See how life works itself out even amid situations that seem wrong? After all, everything happens in its own time.

Adriana Alcântara

Even without saying it, I hope deep down he knew that. A few years later, Talma passed away, and to this day I remember him as a welcoming teddy bear who taught me so much.

When luck happens, courage needs to be on your side

It was winter in New York, but that day was far from charming like the ones you usually see in films and TV shows. It was the kind of cold that made me question everything. Why the hell wasn't I under the Brazilian sun? Instead, I leave the house as if I were an onion with layers and layers of clothes, just to walk with Gigio. That was the name of an English Bulldog that I got on impulse when I arrived in the city.

Gigio didn't ask to be adopted–well maybe he did, just not with words, but with his eyes–and he had to attend to his needs. I couldn't tell if it was because of the cold or because I was in the elevator with a neighbor that I decided not to walk with Gigio on the street that day, but on the terrace, that was in my building. Perhaps it was a mixture of the two. I had seen that lady before, and I knew that she always went to the terrace and let her dog run loose without a leash. She was wearing an *NBC* hat, which made me imagine that she worked or had someone close to her who worked at the network. I figured she could have just bought it as a souvenir, perhaps she was a big fan of the company, but I thought it unlikely.

NBC is one of the largest TV networks in the United States, with international reach. Founded in 1926 as the *National Broadcasting Company*, its headquarters in the *Comcast* Building found in the famous tourist spot of the Rockefeller Center in Manhattan. The channel stood out for its relevance in all segments–news, sports, entertainment, cultural programs–and as a testament to how it was ahead of its time. Sometime before I arrived in New York, a subsidiary of the network known as *MSNBC* was born, the result of a partnership between *Microsoft* and *NBC*. This was in 1996, and they were already starting to build interactivity with the internet, something quite innovative for the time, being a paid 24-hour news platform, whose content was available in Europe, Canada, South Africa, and the Middle East. It was definitely an interesting place to work at.

Connections

I let Gigio off the leash too and went to sit on the same bench as the neighbor. With my good old habit of chatting with everyone, I asked how long she had lived in the building, if she was from New York, and so on. When the topic of conversation changed to me, I told her I had been there for a few months because of my master's degree in communication at NYU, I said that I had several experiences with television in Brazil, and so on. At no point did I ask about her work until she provided the information that I already imagined. She worked at *NBC*.

"Wow, really? Cool! I figured that might be the case because of your hat! You know, I would love it if you could take my resume, as my master's program is ending and it's required to have a year of practical training to complete the course."

The master's degree lasted two years, but I completed some classes earlier so I could fit in a job in case I got an opportunity before graduation.

"Of course, my pleasure!" she replied.

I thanked my neighbor and the overwhelming cold of that day in New York. Remember I said that you often have to make luck happen? In addition to the courage to seize opportunities? My point exactly.

The next day, I stopped by that neighbor's apartment to deliver my resume, and in the same week, *NBC* called me to schedule an interview. I gave my best. I told them about my experience, my expectations, my desires. For someone at that age, I had a lot to tell.

At that network, almost all employees were native English speakers, and those who were not spoke without any accent. Therefore, it wasn't very common for a Brazilian to arrive, with developing English-speaking abilities, in her early twenties, a master's degree, and experience as a host, actress, and screenwriter. But luck, courage, flexibility, and opportunity have always been by my side, and I by theirs.

At *NBC*, I started working on a program called *Headliners and Legends*, hosted by Matt Lauer. It was a documentary-style program about the biography of very symbolic people in the United States–from John F. Kennedy to Clint Eastwood, Bill Gates, and Oprah Winfrey. It covered different types of people: politicians, artists, businesspeople, and athletes, among others. I worked in research and script almost as if returning to the first few months of the *Walking Show*, except this time I had a little more understanding of what I was doing.

As someone who had dealt with so many challenges from Brazilian productions, working on *Headliners* was a dream. Firstly, everything was very easy, in terms of access. *NBC* had a library of videos, articles, and interviews that must have dated back to the invention of the printing press. I remember very well when I worked on actor Michael Douglas' episode and all I had to do was use our system to look up information about him and his father, fellow actor Kirk Douglas. I had at my disposal a collection of files that basically ranged from their entire lives. A surreal number of interviews. Nothing was missing. When we found unlicensed material, we'd purchase the usage rights for the show to avoid any problems in the cash flow. Except for those obituary-style programs, when a celebrity died the next episode had to be about them to get the momentum of the moment. There wasn't that insane pressure or out-of-control hecticness in the *Headliners* production. There was the normal amount of commitment required to the work and the need to do it well.

It was then that I had my first contact with copyright contracts and saw what it was really like to work in the North American market. Punctuality, commitment, professionalism...The meeting started on time and there was no small talk or personal conversations. Time was money, and producing in the best way was the objective. This required total focus from everyone. No one was there to make friends, everyone was going to work and that was that. But a Brazilian is a Brazilian, and I'm me so of course I ended up making good friends there.

The courage to try, to do your best and let the universe take care of the rest

It was 2001, I had been back in Brazil for less than two weeks and I was already questioning why I had returned. There was an unprecedented shock of expectation versus reality. On the personal side, in my naivety, I thought I would find Brazil the way I left it–with single friends, arranging trips, and renting beach houses on the weekend. What I found was everyone was

Connections

married and having children, and I was wondering what I was going to do alone on Saturday night.

On the professional side, I had just finished a great master's degree in New York, worked for *NBC*, one of the top 3 media companies in the United States–I worked in the American division, not the Latin American one. My English was sharpened to a professional level. I lived, studied, worked, and survived New York–which, as Alicia Keys' song says, *"If you can't make it here, you can't make it anywhere."* So, I made it there.

It's not like I expected a badge of honor and a red carpet from the job market, but it also didn't need to be in recession right as I returned. There were no vacancies anywhere. I remember arriving at a company to drop off my resume or to try and have a conversation about a job opportunity, and there'd be a person passing by me crying because they had been let go.

I didn't complain anymore about my return to Brazil, and that my situation was much better in the extremely competitive New York because just under a month later 9/11 happened, placing all problems and their magnitudes in their due places. Everything was fine, I just needed to find my luck. I didn't lack versatility, and at some point, it would work out.

After five months an incredible opportunity arose to debut as a director. It would be a program by Otaviano Costa for *Record*, called *Jogos de Família*. My guardian angel, Fernanda Lauer, continued taking me under her wing even though we were no longer in the recording van of the *Walking Show*. Calling friends from the market, she recommended an opportunity through director Del Rangel. I went in for an interview, and it was great. Del was a nice, direct guy, and I liked him a lot. He was the artistic director of the network *Record*, and since I was quite versatile, the possibilities were good.

A week later, they still hadn't given me a final answer, but the whole thing was going very well. Finally, the investment I made in my resume would have a worthy return. To direct a show on a channel the size of *Record* was quite a responsibility, and I was ready to do whatever was within my reach to create the best show ever seen on Brazilian television. But I was still waiting for *Record*'s response. When the phone finally rang, it was to inform me that Otaviano had been in a car accident which would leave him away from work for months. As of then, the show was canceled.

Again, all the problems and their magnitude were put in their place, and I silenced my questioning about who was actually having bad luck in this situation.

With that, I simply threw in the towel, found the courage I needed, and tried anything. I had my bills to pay, I lived alone, and I wanted to have independence, so I forgot what "weight" my resume had and was willing to take anything that came up. With this, I auditioned as an actress for a soap opera on *SBT*, I auditioned for TV commercials, and I did some corporate films as a host. It was all about swallowing my pride whose first name was "Master's degree at NYU" and whose last name was "employed at *NBC*."

Perhaps the best offer that came my way amid the desert opportunities was Jayme Monjardim's invitation to be his assistant director at *Rede Globo*, but it was in Rio de Janeiro. I had just returned to Brazil after spending years abroad, away from family and friends. Not that things were 100% in São Paulo, but they definitely wouldn't improve in Rio, so I refused. In retrospect, maybe I suffered a little more than necessary, but I felt it was the right decision.

Even though I have a very large network of contacts, it was difficult to get interviews. In the corporate world, we can never take anything for granted because the ferris-wheel spins fast. I joked with a childhood friend, Alê Sousa, son of announcer Silvio Luiz, who practically grew up with me studying at *Pueri Domus*, that I was going to print out my resumes and stick them on city posts or distribute them at traffic lights because I couldn't find a solution. (Always be grateful for the invention of LinkedIn.)

"Can I suggest something?" Alê asked me at one point, and I didn't know whether to say "yes" or "no" because I didn't know if I wanted to hear what he had to say.

"Yes...?"

"Take your master's degree off your resume."

"Why would I do that, Alê?"

To me, the master's degree was the big cherry on top of everything, but Alê argued that my CV scared people.

"You're too young for that resume. You get an interview with a director five or ten years older than you and he doesn't have a master's degree like that. The guy won't want to hire you."

Connections

His point: being young and with a "fear-inducing resume", I could pose a threat to the person who hired me.

"Take it off and see what happens," he suggested.

That's what I did. Alê worked on network TV in Brazil for many years. At one point, he even worked on two at the same time. The guy had a shift at *Record* and another at *SBT*. His opinion was very valid, and that's why I listened to it. Shortly afterward, I got a call. It was about a project that would be filmed in Argentina by a production company called *RGB*, the same one that would later create the extremely successful show *CQC* within a few years. The only reason the project appeared in front of me was because it was going to be recorded practically between Christmas and New Year's Eve, which was when no one wanted to take the work. Even those who didn't have a job already had plans for that time of year. It wasn't my case. My only plan was to find a job.

I was very excited about the project, but I'm not going to spend a single second talking about it here because it was soon canceled after it was born. I don't know why, but I kept thinking that maybe I was the only person who was willing to work at the end of the year. Maybe the production company was unable to form a team to travel to Argentina...What's worth telling is the interaction I had with the person who led the production.

It was Elisabetta Zanetti. Despite Alê's theory having some sense and being supported by the *RGB* connection, Elisabetta certainly wouldn't have felt threatened by my resume. She is a media icon. A beautiful Italian woman who got an MBA in Germany, speaks five languages, and any professional attribute I had, she'd have tenfold. Just to give you an idea, at the moment this book is being written, she is Netflix's number-one person in Brazil, after almost fifteen years of making countless shows with her own production company, *Floresta*, in which Sony was a partner.

All of this was still in the future, but I mention it now to give you context on how a young Adriana Alcântara, returning from the USA and who couldn't even get a job interview wouldn't have intimidated her at all. Below is the best I can remember of my interview. A brief note to set the scene: she interviewed me while breastfeeding her daughter.

"How did you get a work visa in the USA?" she asked, reading the paragraph about my time at *NBC*.

"I did a master's degree, which allowed me to do practical training at the company."

"But that master's degree isn't on your resume."

"I took it off. I was told that someone young like me with a master's degree wouldn't get a job interview."

"I'm not sure about that..."

"But would you be here, talking to me, if I had left the master's degree on there?"

"Probably not, because the opening I have may not live up to the remuneration you expect."

"I have no expectations. I want to prove my worth which is why I took it off my resume."

Looking back and remembering the conversation, what fascinates me is how cold and tired I was, despite desperately wanting a job, and how Elisabetta was extremely professional when dealing with me. She seemed to see that I was hurt by having to hide my qualifications to get a job that might not live up to the investment I made in my professionalization. Maybe she felt my pain, maybe she had already been in my place, maybe she simply acted politely, or perhaps she saw that I could do good work. Of course Alê, who worked at *SBT* and knew Elisabetta, gave me that dash of luck reinforcing that she should give me a chance.

She invited me to a show called *Popstars*, a project between *Disney Channel* and *SBT* to create a reality show about forming a pop music girl band. The judges would be directors from *Sony Music*, which in turn would be the record company that would release the CD, and I signed on to work as a screenwriter.

In 2002, cable TV was gaining strength in Brazil, but almost all of its programming came from abroad and was dubbed. *Popstars* was a New Zealand format, created by Jonathan Dowling, that had already been produced in several countries and became a huge success in Argentina. The idea was to repeat the formula in Brazil. In addition to the main program on *SBT*, there would be a daily program to complement it, which would air on *Disney Channel*.

The show premiered a little earlier than planned on April 27, 2002 on *SBT* as *Globo* had announced the premiere of the rival program, *Ídolos*.

Connections

Silvio Santos being Silvio Santos decided to anticipate *Popstars* so that *Globo* wouldn't get ahead. I remember that while one block was airing, the other was still being edited. The kind of madness that only happens on open TV, and normally in journalism with emergency stories. Although that wasn't the case, it was what happened, and it reminded me of my experience with live journalism at *CNBC*.

Popstars received more than 30,000 entries from girls across the country and only five were selected to join the group, which would later be known as Rouge. Aline Wirley, Fantine Tho, Karin Hils, Li Martins, and Lu Andrade were the winners–being carefully chosen by Sony executives: Liminha, Alexandre Schiavo, Iara Negrete, a vocal coach, and Ivan Santos, who was responsible for physical preparation and for the choreography.

At the end of the project, things took off and I turned one job into another. But it's interesting to think about how it all happened. So many things that seemed to go wrong ended up falling into place. If any piece had moved differently throughout this journey, my story could have been completely different. For example, if after working so hard, I had managed to direct the program with Otaviano Costa, that would have been a huge achievement. But because *Record* is an open TV channel, the program wouldn't necessarily need someone with my background and experience. A range of skills would be important for the position, and perhaps I didn't even have all of them, but the ones I had were not vital for that position.

I could have gotten a job faster, but maybe I would've looked at the professionals around me and wouldn't have connected with them in the same way I did with Elisabetta was a woman of the world whose gaze valued the experience I had and who became an example for me. If I had done the temporary project in Argentina, perhaps it would've blocked the possibility of working on *Popstars*, which was a much longer project with a lot more visibility.

Despite the tears and anguish of having lived through that moment, I learned that persevering in the face of difficulties puts all things in their proper place–the ones we need and the ones we definitely don't need.

To be honest, I say I learned my lesson, but maybe only in theory. In practice... Well, the time will come to tell you more about that. What I want to make clear is that having the courage to face the adversities that arise is essential to moving your energy and getting out of place. The opportunity that appears won't always be perfect for you, but it's worth having the courage to try, to play, to do your best. The universe takes care of the rest.

One way the universe always helps us is by putting the right people in our paths. The key is to identify them and not let the opportunity to connect with them go by. This is how my and Luciana Rodrigues' universes collided back in 2018 when I joined *Cartoon Network*. Since then, in addition to being a great friend, Luciana has become an example of courage, of how to face challenges directly and confidently.

Courage

Luciana Rodrigues

Courage is an act of the heart. I'm not just saying that, it's just the analysis of the etymology of the word.

Courage (n.): from the Latin *coraticum*, it is the association between *cor*, which has as one of its meanings the word "heart", and *aticum*, used to indicate the action of the word that precedes it.

It is the most important of all virtues. Without courage, you cannot practice the others due to the belief that the challenges life imposes are too big. And if there's anything we learn throughout our journey is that there is nothing that comes to us that we cannot tackle.

Living requires courage. But how can we continue if fear is always within us? The Greeks taught us that courage and fear walk hand in hand.

Fear is just a physiological reaction that keeps us on alert and protects us in various circumstances. Without the trigger of fear, we would be in danger. The opposite of courage is not fear, it is cowardice. Fear has its value, but cowardice only serves to hide us from what matters most.

Without courage, there is no evolution. We need it to have the determination to meet the unknown.

In my most recent act of courage, I resigned from a CEO position, crossed the ocean, and moved to a different continent with my family. I can't omit that all this courage came with a breast cancer diagnosis which, ironically, gave me the possibility of pursuing a dream I had reserved for retirement. That is the power of fear.

The day after my mastectomy, I had intense anemia that almost took my life. In that split second, I understood that when the universe gives us a sign, we cannot hesitate. I wasn't throwing away 27 years of a solid career built with a lot of intention and purpose, but instead, I was celebrating a successful journey of lots of learning, failure, frustration, achievement, and growth. Understanding that you are not your title brings liberation.

Khalil Gibran was right about fear transcending when we dare to embrace change and become part of something bigger than ourselves. Just like a river when it meets the ocean, I, Lu Rodrigues, was just embracing my true essence. The river knows that it's not about disappearing into the ocean but becoming the ocean.

Courage is an action, but also a choice.

I wish you the courage to ask, even to strangers on a terrace in New York (thanks for inspiring us, Dri). Courage to accept that we will never be accepted or loved by everyone. Courage to not negotiate your values. Courage to make mistakes. Courage to ask for forgiveness. Courage to forgive. Courage to say "no" when society expects a "yes." Courage to remain, to give up, or to rest when the order is the opposite. Courage to be who you are. Courage to be happy.

The only certainty I have is that every time you dare to take a chance, heaven expands. That's courage.

Luciana Rodrigues is a C-level executive in the communications sector and a columnist for Forbes, mentor, and advisor. She was CEO of *Gray Brasil*, general director of *BuzzFeed*, and vice president of innovations at *Warner Media* for Latin America. Previously, she dedicated her career to some of the most important advertising agencies in the world, where she managed some of the main brands on the Fortune 500 list. With a degree in mediation and conflict management from FGV and in neurosciences and behavior from PUC-RS, her greatest achievement is being a mother to Manuela and Isadora.

Connecting the dots

- More than making luck happen, we need the courage to grab the opportunities that appear on our path. Sometimes we need to be the person who raises their hand and says "I'll do it, leave it to me!", despite the fear.

- Getting out of your comfort zone is painful and gives you butterflies, but that's where the magic is, right on the other side. All you need is the courage to get there.

- To move forward we also need the courage to readjust our route. Adjustments are necessary when we're building our path to success.

- Courage is an action, but also, a choice.

Adriana Alcântara

Now it's your turn!

Courage, like luck and confidence, is fundamental to a successful path and to connect with those who walk alongside us. The good thing is that it is a learnable skill. It's time to strengthen your courage with a simple but powerful reflection exercise, which will give you more confidence to explore the unknown and get out of your comfort zone. The goal here is to show and reinforce to your subconscious that you already have the courage needed, and this way it will be less reluctant when you need to leave your comfort zone again. What haven't you done yet out of fear of making a mistake? What could go wrong and how would it affect you? What lessons would this action bring you, even if it went wrong? Is this action irreversible? Who in your network of connections could help you minimize possible errors? Do you know anyone who has the same desire and could accompany you in this endeavor? Anything goes! Ready?

List below three situations where courage was your biggest ally:

Adriana Alcântara

CHAPTER 4
Flexibility

In 2006, a face-to-face interview would be my last step in the process for a position at *Globosat*. All of the others were done by phone or Skype because I lived in São Paulo and the company was in Rio de Janeiro, more precisely in the neighborhood *Rio Comprido*. They thanked me for coming there for the interview and added that the plan was to move to a new complex, yet to be built in *Barra da Tijuca*. I responded by emphasizing that I was thankful for their interest in me.

With my departure from *Nickelodeon* in the same year, I decided to look for opportunities close to home. Since *Globosat* was on *Avenida Brasil* in São Paulo, less than two miles from where I lived, I figured that it would make sense and I sent in my resume. As an extra push, I asked Carlito Camargo, my former director of the *Walking Show*, if he knew anyone there. He was very close with Wilson Cunha and Leticia Muhana, at the time general directors of *Multishow* and *GNT* respectively. Well, the plan to work close to home didn't go as planned and took me to another state, as the position I would occupy was in Rio de Janeiro.

As we approached the end of the interview, they spoke again about the future change and emphasized that all the windows in the building were protected. The *Rio Comprido* neighborhood had its risks. Rio de Janeiro has its dangers and, from time to time, the region suffered from shootings and the building had to be evacuated in a hurry.

I found the emphasis on the location interesting because I didn't come from Switzerland, but from São Paulo, which in 2006 had witnessed many days of terror with organized crime. In order to alleviate their concern,

Connections

I said everything was fine. I even mentioned that I had lived in Iraq during a war to try to alleviate their worries.

It was July 1987. I don't know how many hours had passed, maybe a million. First stop in Paris, then Baghdad. But finally, we arrived. As expected, the reality check happened right there, in the airport lobby. I was inside a movie. The place was beautiful and modern, with mirrors and glass that somehow kept the heat of the desert on the outside. But what I noticed were the people sitting on the floor, despite there being plenty of seats available. Entire families sitting in a circle, men in turbans carrying in their hands some type of rosary (which I would later learn was called *masbaha*), and women wearing burqas trying to control children (children will always be children anywhere on this planet). Important: men talking to men and women taking care of their children. Each one plays their part and is very separated, respecting the religion. A very clear difference in Islamic culture is this separation of tasks between men and women. Putting it in perspective, even with the equality challenges we have in Brazil, which were even more significant at that time, the shock is still inevitable.

I should have asked myself why it was the women who had to cover their entire bodies, or what was the reason for women to always have to walk a few steps behind their male counterparts when a more urgent problem arose for a western thirteen-year-old teenage girl than imagining a cultural revolution in a context that she hadn't had contact with yet:

"Mom, where's my suitcase?"

Unlike what would perhaps be expected of any girl at this age, when my mother informed me that we were moving with my stepfather to Iraq, I was excited. But in my mother's typical way the phrase "we're going to live in Baghdad" wasn't a notification to prepare us psychologically for something that would occur within a few months. Instead, it was closer to: "Pack your bags because we're moving in two weeks." During this period, we got the mandatory vaccines for the trip and some medical tests. Due to the speed at which everything happened, all we could take was exactly one suitcase of clothes–the rest would be left behind.

Adriana Alcântara

Amid a war that was ravaging the country, the possibility of shipping furniture in a container and its arrival didn't exist. The only option was to let go of everything and move forward with what could fit in just one suitcase. But of course, since I'm the oldest and on top of that a girl, I didn't want to mix my things with my brothers' or my little sister Elora, who was just three years old. The result: the airline lost precisely the only suitcase that contained the clothes of the teenager who was going to live in an Arab country. It wasn't like I could just buy new clothes. The women's fashion market in Iraq was one of the simplest in the world: women wore burqas, nothing else. I was willing to embrace a little of the local culture, but to do so right away on the first day was asking a lot! On top of that, the local heat was infernal, and black burqas did not facilitate adaptation to the temperature. To me, it was like wearing a suit in a 104° Rio summer.

In 1987, there were still no baggage tracking systems or any of the technological ease we enjoy today, which allows this type of stress to be alleviated. At that time, all we could do was wait for the airline to notify the airport about the loss of the suitcase and hope that it hadn't been sent to the other side of the world. But considering that my current location was Baghdad, it was best to not get any hopes up. In the end, the quickest solution was to buy a burqa, and my mother used a sash she had as a belt to pretend it was a little dress. It didn't work, my mind and my heart were not deceived. It goes back to that phrase that no one likes to hear, but no one has ever disagreed with: "What has no solution is solved."

In reality, the local people were going through so much adversity that my problem was completely ridiculous. Iraq, in 1987, was in the midst of a war against Iran. However, as a teenager who had just left most of her life behind, including her father, the situation was disappointing.

I do not intend to delve into the intricacies of 1980s geopolitics, but as a form of contextualization: Saddam Hussein, dictator of Iraq, had decided to invade the neighboring country of Iran on the account of ancient territorial conflicts. Maybe they thought that everything would be resolved in a few weeks or months, but that's not how it went. And seven years later, when we landed in Baghdad, the two sides were still fighting and there were no signs of an end to the conflict. Brazil became a character in all of this due to the whims of history.

Connections

Just a year before I was born, the world went through one of its greatest cataclysms: the oil crisis. The cartels of countries that produced the commodity decided to increase the oil price, and nothing could be done. When the value of a barrel of oil quadrupled, Brazil was the seventh largest importer–the other six were rich countries. One of the solutions found for the pandemonium that occurred in Brazil–which used almost half of its exports just to pay the oil bill–was to start the *Pró-Álcool* program, in which national technology developed an alternative to gasoline, through the use of ethanol as fuel. But Brazil, although large, didn't have enough alcohol to meet the country's demand. As said in the cliché, which must have been said by a Brazilian: "Every crisis is an opportunity."

The thought process: due to the value of oil continuing to be high even with some decreases over the years, Iraq had endless financial reserves. But everything else was missing from the country, from food and manufactured products to infrastructure. These were things that Brazil could offer, so the two countries sat down to talk. We soon became Iraq's third-largest trading partner, and the main sector that benefited was civil construction. The company Mendes Júnior, a big name in construction work in Brazil, signed the biggest contract for a national company abroad up to now: 1.3 billion dollars to build the railway that connected the city of Akashat to the capital of the country, Baghdad.[5]

The commercial honeymoon between the two countries, especially for Brazilian companies, began to decline due to an event that took everyone by surprise, despite its predictability: a war with the neighboring country. From then on, Iraq stopped fulfilling its financial obligations to the Brazilians, to the point that it reached International litigation. It was at that moment in history that a little Dri Alcantara went to Baghdad.

When I was eight years old, my mother remarried. His name was Attila de Sousa Leão Andrade Jr., a second father to me. They met on a cruise, and after a few months of dating, he moved from Rio de Janeiro to São Paulo so that the two could get married in a ceremony, in which I was the bridesmaid. A few years later, my sister Elora was born. With the arrival

---

[5] László Varga, "Antes das guerras, país era parceiro comercial do Brasil". Folha de S. Paulo, April 20, 2003. Available at: <https://www1.folha.uol.com.br/fsp/dinheiro/fi2004200307.htm>. Accessed on:: Sept. 21, 2024.

of Attila, the day-to-day life in our house began to include gatherings spoken in a foreign language, always with lots of music–he played the piano divinely–and fun. This fit my mother's predisposition to welcome guests and her versatility in languages and instruments like a glove (my mother played the piano, guitar, and accordion). It must have been around that time I started to marvel at the universe of foreign languages. When my stepfather and my mother wanted to talk without us understanding what they were saying, they spoke in French, and I thought that was incredible. I also believe that it was a way to demonstrate how important it was to study and be fluent in other languages–at the very least, this allows you to know if anyone is badmouthing you right in front of you.

This appetite for the international that Attila had generated several trips with my mother, some of them lasting months since he was often invited to teach as a guest professor at several universities around the globe. He was a leader in the international law world and the author of many books on the subject that were translated into several languages. It was an interesting combination to see this guy with a unique intellect, extremely scholarly, have this other side to him. He sometimes felt like a young traveler without roots, suitcase always packed and ready for a new adventure. And it was in Iraq that these two veins converged.

Mendes Júnior's work to build the railway began in September 1978 and was to be handed over to the Iraqi government in 1983. That's exactly what happened. However, halfway through, the war began, and with no end in sight, the country stopped paying its dues to invest in its military. The war dragged on as did the Iraqi's debt. It was at this moment that the company summoned a legion of lawyers with experience in private international law to seek a solution. Our dad Attila was invited to lead them.

It's not difficult to understand why he agreed to move with four kids to a country still at war. In terms of comparison, it's as if today's Dubai was Baghdad back then. To them, the idea of an international experience with people from all over the world was very attractive. It was something you only imagined you'd see and learn about in textbooks. At the same time, there was a cosmopolitan city next door sponsored by oil money.

Fortunately, we had the privilege of living in a safe area, a very different reality in many places. From our apartment in Baghdad, we could

Connections

hear the bombs, but strangely, we were not afraid for our safety. I think that when we are in a situation, after a while it's normalized. It just becomes your reality.

After ten years in the country, Mendes Júnior offered all kinds of security guarantees for its expatriates in Iraq. What came in the package was a house, an international school, and access to a small market that brought goods in from Brazil. There was never anything perishable available because the trip to stock up our private grocery store was long. In the city, it was very difficult to find fresh fruit, which changed our routine a lot because we were an economically privileged family from Brazil that always had fruits at home. My mother has always been a fan of a good farmer's market and freshly squeezed juices. In Baghdad, this was impossible.

Looking around, everything was different–the landscape, the buildings, and the food which brought complications. We sometimes didn't know what we were eating because we didn't speak Arabic, and they didn't speak English. With the goodwill of the local people and lots of miming, we managed. The only extremely delicate thing was for a woman to walk alone. Culturally this demonstrated a huge difference from the reality I was accustomed to.

The situation with the lost suitcase (which appeared after a month of waiting) and the food brought some reflections on how access to basic conditions can be so different. Brazil is a country of sad contrasts. With everyday life, we would end up being swallowed up by routine, and we would reflect less than we should on the subject. Iraq put me in touch with something I had never experienced: the lack of availability of the things I used to have access to within my privileged life. This may have been my biggest shock, even more so than the different customs and culture. It wasn't like we could go shopping. Even with the privilege of having the conditions to buy things, there was nothing for sale. No money in the world can buy something that doesn't exist–which inevitably made me reflect on the privileged scenario in which I was born and raised.

In circumstances like this, two things happen. The first is universal and inescapable: human beings discover their flexibility, adapt, and get used to their circumstances–good thing because that's how humanity got this far. The second thing is personal because, unlike the first, it's a choice. In the

Adriana Alcântara

absence of the reality we are accustomed to, it is possible to become more compassionate and empathetic, as if a sense of collectivity took over to help get through that situation.

During the flight, my mother met a woman named Stéphanie, whose Brazilian husband already lived and worked in Iraq as CEO of Volkswagen. She was traveling with her daughter Ana, who was more or less my age. On the plane, I remember I admired Ana when she spoke to the flight attendants in very well-tuned English. I thought I would soon have the same dexterity. As we headed to Baghdad, we talked about what to expect in Iraq and things like that, creating the type of relationship that generally lasts for the duration of a flight. I was already focused on making connections while living in a place where I knew a lot of people, so I figured I'd be great at living in a place where I didn't know anyone or speak the language.

While we waited for our bags and everyone picked up their own, it became increasingly evident that mine had not traveled with us. Two days later, without any kind of confirmation that my clothes would appear in Baghdad, my mother had an idea: in addition to her age, Ana was also about my size. We decided to make a visit to her home and try our luck. I eventually left there with two pairs of shorts, three T-shirts, and a pair of sweatpants with the clothes I wore on the trip together, making up my wardrobe.

It's important to note that she wasn't just lending me clothes. From the moment she passed her suitcase to me, Ana gave me something impossible to replace. To help someone, she let something go. She became flexible so that another person could be helped. They were just insignificant clothes, I know, but a simple favor gains another level of relevance and meaning. That was the lesson that, despite not rationalizing it completely at the time, I managed to internalize. Helping others is good for the soul. No matter how ridiculous my frustration was, I had help. Once again, a privilege.

Connections

Flexibility to accept opportunities that come our way and deal with challenges

As I said at the beginning of the chapter, moving to a different city was not a part of my plan. I had just moved to a new apartment in São Paulo, and I even had it renovated to fit my style. As a very fortunate person and just as my father fully supported me in my move to New York, he also helped me with the move to Rio de Janeiro. He looked into getting a bigger apartment so he and other family and friends could come visit me, helping me feel less alone. We looked at our options together and finally, we found one in *Ipanema* that met our needs. Yes, I know, a luxury of the few. Thank you, Dad, for always encouraging me and accompanying me.

In addition to the upheaval of moving and restructuring a whole life in Rio de Janeiro–although not so far from São Paulo isn't exactly easy–the job itself required me to step out of my comfort zone.

Even though I loved a challenge, and had never avoided one in my career, my work has always been within the production universe. Entering *Globosat*'s programming acquisitions department, the scope would be to seek content for the company's various channels in international markets. At the time, there was no law requiring a quota of national content on paid TV channels (it was already being discussed, but would only be approved in 2011). So, it was possible to set up programming by buying content from other markets, the famous "canned goods". We'd just have to subtitle and dub the shows to have a channel ready to go.

That's what attracted me: the opportunity to work in an area that I didn't know much about and opening a window to the world while expanding my knowledge. I had to search for shows from around the world– coming from the USA, the United Kingdom, Argentina, Canada, France, or Australia–that could be interesting for different *Globo* subscription channels and negotiate to acquire products in the most profitable way possible. This required making many international contacts and traveling the world in search of the best options.

A good example of these negotiations was *Super Nanny* from the *BBC*, which had several seasons, some in England and others in the United States. There were also international gastronomy programs, such as Jamie

Adriana Alcântara

Oliver's. The international sale of these products normally occurs when they have already aired in their countries of origin, and often, the sales price is linked to audience success. With this challenge, I discovered a new part of the TV universe that I didn't even know existed.

In addition to traveling, I needed to familiarize myself with and create creative business models and large-volume contracts. Things that were very far from my comfort zone. My experience helped when it came to the numbers as I had an idea of how much the shows cost, which gave me a competitive advantage. At the same time, I needed to have a very intense internal interface when having constant meetings with the teams from *GNT*, *Multishow*, *Telecine*, and *Sportv*. I ended up gaining a lot of visibility because I interacted with almost all of the Globosat teams. My thirst for creating connections with the greatest possible number of people and my flexibility to adapt to different personalities made a difference once again. At *Globosat*, I met lots of interesting people who became dear friends, references, and even valuable connections in my professional world, such as Daniela Mignani, Bruna Demaison, Carolina Iacia, and Eduardo Leal.

The people who worked in the acquisitions department had been created there through internal opportunities. Such as the analyst had once been an intern, and the junior coordinator would be promoted to senior, a position that the supervisor had previously occupied. Maybe I was the first person who arrived with a rich market history having experience in other companies, and I was very well received by everyone because they saw the value in my vision. These new ideas came accompanied by challenges, and questions that were not previously common. By having an outsider with a background in different areas, I could bring new perspectives and offer different references. This dynamic caused some obstacles in my relationship with my boss. Previously, everyone who worked in that department had learned from her. I arrived with a past that could either generate evolution or confusion.

My direct team couldn't be better, which made for a very fun day-to-day. First, Carolina Iacia, a sweet girl who welcomed me as soon as I arrived. At the time of the beginning of her journey, she gave me a ride every day from where we lived in *Ipanema*, to *Rio Comprido*. We became so close that I met her entire family, who were obviously the foundation behind all

Connections

her politeness, compassion, and kindness. Then, there was Eduardo Leal. At the time, he was also at the beginning of his career, and like Carol, was a super-prepared guy with a heart of gold. Edu had a priceless sense of humor. Together, we had fun, supported each other, and learned a lot.

Even with the tranquility we created, the dynamics of the department with management were not very easy and required a lot of flexibility. There were communication failures, and the manner direction was given was not constructive, which generated discontent. Leadership didn't connect with the team openly, so there was no room for ideas and opinions to flow and contribute to the evolution of everyone on the team. As my position reported to the director and there was a team beneath me, I was stuck in the middle trying to find a common denominator.

At work, we always encounter personalities in which we connect with and others that are more challenging. I believe this leadership period developed my flexibility. It was not easy even with having experience and knowing everything I could contribute, but not being able to change anything. Even with the obstacles, I was evolving and learning a new skill, with Carol and Edu by my side making everyday life light and worthwhile.

After a few months, the company decided to do a group exercise conducted by a consultant to assess leadership profiles. In this activity, each group would have fifty participants, but in the end, those with the strongest leadership tendencies within each group would be identified. After three days of activities, 48 people voted for me–the only differing votes being from myself, as I nominated another person in the group and someone who voted for themselves.

I found this very fascinating. I felt like I didn't do much, but it turns out that I actually acted as a leader by organizing the ideas and bringing together opinions so that as a group we could perform well. It's astonishing how important communication is and how it makes us stand out in a crowd. Sometimes you don't know more than someone else, but if you're able to express your point concisely and clearly with the right amount of information and details that prove it without losing your audience's attention, your message will be transmitted more effectively. If you have all the information to prove a point but express it confusingly, you won't prove your argument and no one will understand your vision. It's similar to the way we learn to articulate texts in school. An essay must have a beginning, middle, and end. The middle needs to defend its conclusion in an organized and coherent manner.

The interesting thing was that, during the activity, no one–directors, managers, interns–could reveal what position they held. Somehow because of my personality of taking initiative and engaging with the proposal, I ended up standing out. When I went to receive individual feedback from the HR director, also having the presence of my boss, the group had defined me as a *Romário*, or a *Ronaldinho*. Two famous Brazilian soccer players who were known for being great team leaders.

"But your manager doesn't see you that way, Adriana."

"It turns out that when a Ronaldinho or a Romário comes onto the field, he knows which way to run and which goal to shoot at because of the color of the shirt he wears. But if you put him in the game without clearly identifying which team he's a part of, there's no point in being a star. Before the match starts there is already a 50% chance of things going wrong."

They looked at me as if I had spoken Greek.

"I have difficulty understanding my manager's strategy and direction. I don't know how she expects me to act," I concluded. I developed this analogy by using many words when one was enough. The conversation turned to my communication–or rather the lack of efficiency in it.

"You must be struggling to express yourself and make yourself understandable to your manager," the HR director said, adding that she would include in my final evaluation a suggestion for me to attend an acting class.

It was my turn to look at her in disbelief. I had stood out "just" by listening to everyone and various points of view to reach a better decision for the group, but they were claiming that my manager was 100% right, and I was 100% wrong. Don't issues of clarity and communication always include at least two people or more? HR found it more productive to put the problem completely on me rather than using this conversation as an opportunity to improve communication between my manager and me. I thought that was unfair to her, to me, and to the company, which had invested a lot in that activity.

Connections

"And what class do you suggest I take? I am a professional actress, who graduated from the Lee Strasberg Institute, in New York. I've worked in two soap operas, three miniseries, and three plays."

It was a very acidic, very wrong, and very arrogant response, but it was compatible with my hot head at that moment. I couldn't understand how, even after an assessment where I managed to communicate well enough with 49 strangers to the point of becoming the leader of the group, the problem was still me! On top of that, they were suggesting a solution that wouldn't help anyone evolve–neither me nor my boss. Much less our work dynamic. That conversation was a waste of time. I kept asking myself if HR, with all its experience, actually believed that the suggestion was valid. That it would lead to a better relationship between us and better results for the company.

Ultimately that feedback did nothing. I had already tried to switch to another department, and there was no shortage of invitations, but as "bad" as I was, my boss wouldn't let me leave. There was an internal practice where the current manager had to agree for the professional to migrate to another department. Although unfair, it was how it worked. All I could do was become more flexible every day and continue to look on the bright side of that challenge. I was learning to negotiate with people from all over the world and familiarizing myself with content from countless international entertainment markets. Focusing your thoughts on the positive reduces the relevance of the negative and raises your energy. When we focus on the negative, it seems like we go to work with a hundred pounds on our shoulders and just surviving the hours at the office becomes difficult and tiring.

When a new challenge arrived, I resigned. My manager invited me to dinner, and it was the first time in almost two years of working together that we saw each other outside the work environment. To me, it was a very natural practice, but it had never happened with her. There was no opening for me to suggest something like that. Even on the trips we took together, she would be on a separate flight, stay in another hotel, and have dinner with contacts I didn't have access to. After almost two years of working directly together, I knew absolutely nothing about her story, way of thinking, priorities, challenges, and much less her weaknesses or frustrations.

We talked candidly and, surprisingly, she opened up to me. She said she was shy and had trouble expressing her thoughts in a conversation, which is why she ended up giving orders instead of discussing possibilities because it was easier for her. I found it very genuine. She also pointed out that she saw in me a lot of the preparation she had at my age. It's interesting because I consider myself quite open and communicative, but I saw it as a compliment. After all, she had been the director of Globosat for many years.

This experience taught me flexibility and empathy. To understand that not everyone has the same ability to communicate or the same view on things, and sometimes, the content is compromised due to the way it's presented. While she had difficulty listening and changing the way she sees things, I confess that I didn't have the emotional intelligence to deal with that relationship. Today, I would've had the proactiveness to open up to her about my weaknesses, and, who knows, maybe she'd open up back. At the time, I was intimidated by the barrier she placed, so I stood further and further away, as if knocking down that wall was impossible. The lesson I learned at that dinner: it is never impossible to connect.

The conversation was great and a necessary closure for me to leave with this lesson. I feel sorry we didn't have the same opportunity at the beginning of my story at *Globosat*, as perhaps things would have been different. But at that time I was worn out, and it was time for a change, which came from a recommendation within the company: Daniela Mignani, at the time manager of *Multishow*'s marketing department.

Back to Baghdad

After years with Mendes Júnior in the country, it was no surprise that there was a considerably large community of Brazilians in Iraq. It was divided between the families of engineers, who lived in villages set up close to the construction sites and had schools that taught classes in Portuguese for their children, and the families of employees in administrative areas of the company, who lived in the capital–this was our case.

One of the conditions imposed by my mother and Attila, and perhaps something that justified taking us to Baghdad, was to study at an

Connections

international school: The Baghdad International School, or BIS. It was located next to the United Nations building in Iraq, and this brought a certain security to the place. This UN building had a shelter underground which we constantly practiced running to in case something happened–such as bombs flying towards Baghdad. In fact, during one of these trainings that took place suddenly but recurrently, I was in the bathroom and I didn't hear the alarm go off. When I returned to the classroom no one else was there. I knew what was happening, but before I could head to the shelter, a teacher came running desperately to get me. When I arrived outside, the whole school was looking at me. It was embarrassing, and I remember to this day how I felt. I had only been at the school for a short time, and my communication was still very compromised. I didn't feel good about the entire school seeing me in such a vulnerable position.

This was a school where only the children of expatriates studied. The only Iraqis there were the children of diplomats, perhaps as a way of carrying out some type of international integration for when they'd eventually move to another country. It was the only exception. But regardless of where I was enrolled, I would have to get by in English. When I was thirteen years old, my understanding of the language came more from listening to foreign music than from the classes in school.

There were no support classes in English, so the idea was simply to learn as you go. In elementary school, there was the normal school program and then there was an additional hour of studying for those who weren't fluent. But at the high school, it was assumed that you were already fluent, which was far from being my case. Add this to an array of different accents, ranging from Japanese with its confusing consonants, to Italian which was so melodic that you couldn't differentiate a question from a statement. We were in the most perfect modern representation of the Tower of Babel–which was in Iraq.

It was quite strange to me at first, like many other things I encountered there. How could I, the person whose middle name is "communication," not say anything beyond *Good morning* and *How are you*? In a way, everyone there was experiencing an international school for the first time and shared the same challenges. Everyone had to dance to the music, without knowing the choreography, so we managed as best we could.

Adriana Alcântara

We were a bunch of teenagers who had been thrown to the lions, and each day we learned to tame our embarrassments and frustrations through the barrier of cultural differences. In the end, with patience and a lot of miming on my part, it became fun.

It was exactly this mixture of cultures and experiences that I enjoyed the most. Where else could I learn something about France, Australia, and Romania, while living in an Arab country, all on the same day? Everyone I talked to had an interesting story to tell. In addition to being natives of different places, they had all lived in several foreign countries. They talked about their cultures, but also, how they adapted and learned in each place they lived. It's interesting to think about how culture ends up dictating our way of speaking and the words we choose, no matter the language. Culture permeates our palate, our clothing, and even the sports we enjoy. More than anything, culture shapes our way of relating to those around us.

One of the funniest and most surreal situations happened when it was announced that there would be a school talent show. There was a group of girls who liked ballet, and owning pointe shoes was true proof of our love for dance. We got together and decided that our performance would be a classical ballet number. One day, one of the girls in the group called my home. I don't remember her name or nationality. She said her pointe shoes were too small and she wanted to switch with me. She argued that we wore the same size, so my shoes would fit her perfectly. I responded that if we wore the same size, and her shoes were tight, they would also be tight on me. Her response was simply: "No, Adriana, they're going to be fine on your feet."

This back and forth over such an obvious thing lasted for a few minutes, and I tried to defend myself with my still very poor English–Attila laughed beside me as he listened to the conversation in disbelief. I don't know what she was thinking. Maybe she thought the Brazilian in the group would be the easiest to deceive, or maybe she actually believed in the "two plus two equals three" that she tried to convince me of. Either way, it was a mistake. At the same time, I understood her dilemma. I had experienced it myself a few months ago before my suitcase finally showed up. It wasn't like she could go to a store and find the perfect pair of pointe shoes. And this

Connections

talent show was a unique occurrence. In a community where everything revolved around school, almost all family programs, birthday parties, and smaller events were with the same people who frequented that environment. In terms of entertainment, there was no theater, cinema, amusement parks, or even common parks. The relationships formed were niched in that space in which the international school orbited.

We had been living in Iraq, but it was still a foreign country to us. So, when a talent show came up, which would only happen once a year, everyone wanted to participate and deliver the best performances possible. Was it a small deal? Yes. But that's what we had.

I also know that just a few months earlier I met a sweet girl who gave me her clothes in a moment of necessity. Even in a situation like that– having the opportunity to participate in the event of the year, after all, what else could we expect to happen in terms of fun in wartime Iraq?–I would've lent my pointe shoes if she came up with a story like: "My mother is leaving and we won't see each other for years, and I wanted to give her this ballet performance as a farewell gift." Yes. If it was something on that level or more tragic, I would've given up my shoes. But here we had this European who came up with an impossible argument, trying to out-smart the Brazilian.

Anyway, me being me, I agreed to try that exchange to see if it could work, but her shoe wouldn't fit my foot at all. I then offered my regular ballet shoes, which I had also packed, and placed the ribbons around her ankle, just like you would with pointe shoes. As I learned from my mother on the day of the burqa "dress", creativity can help minimize the challenges of our reality and make things happen joyfully. I always tell my daughter that life is easier when we work with solutions. That way we were all able to dance together with a packed audience, on an unforgettable night in the center of Baghdad.

I was aware of the privilege I experienced. I didn't know anyone else who had that opportunity. Despite missing home and friendships in Brazil, the fact is that, at thirteen years old, the most I was missing out on were birthday parties. It wasn't like I was in my early twenties, traveling to the beach on the weekends with my group of friends. Still, at the end of the day, I missed my friends. What I wanted most was to be able to get home, pick up the phone, and call each of them to tell them about my day. But it wasn't possible. That was Iraq at war. Saddam Hussein's government completely controlled communication. The few families that had a telephone at home, like us, were only able to make local calls. It was impossible to make an international call. For example, I remember on September 8th, my dad's birthday, we had to make an appointment at the Brazilian embassy to call him from there. We scheduled it two months in advance. The interesting thing was that I could tell how my father, born in 1941, liked to talk about how phone calls were made back in "his day": you had to call the operator and coordinate everything, schedule a specific time for the person to return to the device, and then complete the call. After this experience, the value we give to being able to talk to someone at any time changes.

The other option for external communication was through letters, but they also had their restrictions. The government intercepted everything. I believe that during the war period, there wasn't a single letter deposited in the Iraqi mailbox that wasn't immediately read by an Iraqi agent. And as they had no shame in hiding what they did–nothing like the movie scenes of a spy using the vapor of a kettle to open an envelope without leaving a trace– the result was that most of these letters never reached their destination. They were either censored, or the snooping damaged the envelope to the point that the letter ended up lost.

The solution for us Brazilians: use Mendes Júnior and its pouch of correspondence that left Baghdad once a month for São Paulo without going through the curious eyes and inept fingers of Saddam Hussein's spies. The same happened on the other side. When my friends wanted to write to me, they had to take it to the Mendes Júnior office by a certain day, so it would join the company's monthly mailbag in time. During my entire time in Iraq, this is how I communicated with my friends–which was a great loss for the Iraqi agents, as they were the most beautiful and multicolored letters that anyone can imagine. Stickers, drawings with colored pencils, neon markers, and anything else the paper could hold.

As I had chosen to take Arabic classes as well, I always wrote their names in the language. It was a very 1980s teenager kind of thing, but it felt

Connections

like being in 1880. It was roughly a three-month gap between the time we'd write the letters and receive a response. The news we read about each other was already in the past. The gossip that happened at a birthday party in August, I heard about in November. The cool, caring, handsome boy that one of them had fallen in love with had turned into a boring, not-so-handsome jerk, just three months later.

Locally, I ended up getting close to Sara from Scotland, who was in my class. Coincidentally, she lived in the same building as me, in the Al Mansur neighborhood. The building had two towers and a swimming pool in the middle which we often went to on weekends. There were only foreigners living in this building, and therefore the use of bikinis was permitted. For some time, my life was summed up between home and school, until we became members of the British Club, which also had a swimming pool, and nothing else. Even so, it was good to break up the routine a little on the weekends. Ana, who lent me the clothes, was also a member there, so I had someone my age to talk to.

I also gained more friends from other grades when my mother became the school's music teacher–both for my year and the upperclassmen. My mother is also a lawyer, but my grandparents made her study everything. She speaks various languages and plays different instruments, which for a country at war was more than enough to achieve that role. She never lacked flexibility, and when she saw the opportunity, she seized it.

Flexibility to adjust the route and follow new paths

Even though I loved the role I played at *Globosat*, I didn't see an opportunity for growth there, especially in the department I was in. I made friends at all channels, people who accompany me to this day, a network of connections with incredibly competent professionals with enormous relevance in the market. Even so, I decided to leave, and I think this was one of the few times I made a thoughtful career move because I decided to test my flexibility on the other side of the counter.

Someone I met, and who became my greatest friend, was Daniela Mignani, marketing manager at *Multishow*. She was married to José Luis

Volpini who, at that moment, was setting up the operation to launch *Oi TV*, a paid satellite TV service from the telecommunications company *Oi*. I had already met Volpini, as we were neighbors in *Ipanema*. Daniela recommended me because she believed I had an interesting range of experiences for the position: production, negotiation, both national and international, and my communication and leadership attributes. I was also already in Rio, which was one less headache (and expense).

Who wouldn't want to participate in the creation of a television operation? That magical place where everything is possible...Well, if only the theory was the same as the practice...I came from companies that focused on emotional selling, where the content and projects only generated profit through the emotional connection of the public with the product. But at *Oi*, no one wanted to waste a lot of time on emotions. It was all based on "How much does it cost?", "How much will you charge?", "What's the margin?"– a more rigid DNA guided by numbers, with the objective of them being blue, as a positive sign and in reflection of constant growth. A male-dominated company, as I imagine all companies and engineering programs to be.

Don't get me wrong. Every company exists to make a profit, I agree. This is what justifies its existence, and everything else just orbits around this reason. Even though I've typically been more involved in the playful side of things, I always understood that it only happens if it's supported by positive business results. I even dedicated myself to a master's degree to prepare to manage a business plan in all its complexity. But that would be the first time that I'd be responsible for reconciling these two spectrums, and I soon understood that it would not cause any change being the revolutionary humanities person in the pure world of STEM. I would need to adjust my speech to a different audience than I have worked with throughout the past twenty years of my career.

It was necessary to learn to stick to each argument about how a program connects to the public, and the profitability it can bring. When it was time to talk about the potential of a project because of the behavioral tendencies, you had to also present conversion estimates. As I learned to navigate those waters, I gained a gratifying internal feeling of genuine happiness that motivated me even more because it was all very challenging to me. I didn't know anything about that world, and in these situations, we

Connections

need to be strategic and flexible. It was important to demonstrate vulnerability, but it had to come alongside the value I added. After all, they hired me because I knew something, and that needed to balance out what I didn't know.

As soon as I arrived, I confess that I felt overwhelmed by shyness because it was the first time I was leading such a large direct team. In the first meeting, everyone put their cell phones on the table, and in 2008, this was still seen as a sign of disrespect in my old corporate world. I later understood that in Telecom this is the typical practice. No one had landlines so cell phones were an extension of the human body.

The team was sharp. By coincidence of fate, among the members, there was Bruna Demaison, who left *Globosat* for *Oi* a few months before me. Bruna helped me disseminate TV culture in a team that came with other experiences and was also in the same boat as me, trying to learn skills I didn't have. Months after my arrival, a role became available, and I brought my faithful *Globosat* shield, Carolina Iacia. After a few years through an interview process, I met Carolina Andrade, who left the channel *Brasil* to join us. I didn't meet her at *Globosat*, but at *Oi*. She came at the right time for the right job, and she was the one who ran things during my maternity leave. Besides them, other people took turns filling vacancies at *Oi*. The company's structure changed every six months, which meant a new boss and a new team. When everything was fine, we knew it could get worse soon. When it was bad, we knew it would change soon, but it couldn't get any worse.

I had a team with a lot of experience in navigating *Oi*, but little experience in content creation in any format. At the time, the area known as value-added services (VAS) made a fortune selling ringtones, wallpapers for cell phones, horoscope services, and other unimaginable things in today's world. I lost a few night's sleep at the beginning of my days at *Oi*. There were so many acronyms that I thought I'd never feel at home. The worst thing is that I had no one to call because my network of contacts was not from this world either. Therefore, I had to fend for myself and find a formula for success. Because almost nobody had worked in TV, the way forward was to first show them what I knew to then balance it out by sharing my weaknesses.

Adriana Alcântara

The only content that existed on *Oi* at the time was "*Oi Futuro*," the company's institute that financed cultural projects, such as the *Rio de Janeiro Film Festival* and the *Rio Content Market*, which only got off the ground thanks to *Oi* TV's investment in the first edition. But this was so far removed from our reality that it was located in another building. It was a big challenge to bring a less rigid perspective to an emotional sale within a company like *Oi*.

A family subscribes to paid TV because they want to spend time together watching a movie. They want their children to have options for children's programming at any time during the day. Through TV they can visit other countries and discover new worlds that are often impossible to visit in person. The sale of *Oi* TV was, in fact, the sale of the channels that were available within it, and not the sale of the equipment. No one chooses their TV service based on which box is prettier. Not to mention that *Oi* TV was *Oi*'s first product with partners. In practice, each channel that was in the *Oi* TV packages received a monthly payment transfer and also approved all promotions and communications. The other products that *Oi* sold were 100% owned by the company.

It was a challenge for little me–Adriana Alcântara, 5'4'' and 110 pounds, to sit next to the board of directors, made up only of men accustomed to products that are much more tangible than the sale of subscription TV. But as I gained credibility, I gained their trust without deepening my voice or using huge high heels to increase my height. This way, I motivated myself even more and was immensely happy. Not because I was being validated by the men but because I was able to overcome my own initial limitations. In the end, I learned a lot from them and their management models and experience. I gained a good balance of technical for my very humanities-based brain.

However, it is also necessary to highlight a very differentiating factor, Volpini, who was great and empowered me so much throughout this process. I remember a specific meeting in Miami, with *HBO*, which was a very difficult negotiation. All of the channel's Latin American leaders were Mexicans, Venezuelans, and other Latinos, less accustomed to female leadership. It took a lot of flexibility to make it happen. So much so that a

Connections

time came when I said that it would be better for Volpini to lead the rest of the conversation, as we were running the risk of sinking the deal.

He went with me to this specific meeting because I insisted, on the good of the company. But, being there, with all those men only interacting with him, Volpini remained silent, only opening his mouth to say: "That's up to Adriana, she's the one who will decide."

He made a point of putting me in a place of relevance. He was the boss who empowered me the most and did so in a way that was kind to me and others. I have immense gratitude and infinite memories of our coexistence and the breezy way in which we tackled challenges and goals that were quite heavy. Our day-to-day life was fun, funny, and fluid even at a company full of pressure and demand for results. I learned a lot from him.

It was a shame that the recognition of my work–and of my person– had to come from his account. Any movement to empower a woman contributes to seeking a better balance in leadership roles. I am very lucky to have had this possibility, which I made a point of replicating as I climbed to higher positions in my trajectory.

I have often reflected on 2024 and the year I lived in Iraq–not only from my experience but from what I could observe in a country where scarcity is the norm. Being able to adapt is the difference. What is not flexible will break under pressure. My time at *Globosat* and *Oi TV* made me think about those adolescent days because there I was, in many ways, far from my zone of comfort. But when we are willing to stand outside of it, we find magic. By being flexible, we may be surprised at how much we can endure and how much further we can go.

Flexibility

Daniela Mignani

"The only constant in life is change."
Heraclitus, a Greek philosopher

Adriana Alcântara

Why is it so difficult to change?

Change is mourning. Symbolic mourning. Because we abandon a set of actions, achievements, feelings, learning, and experiences that we will eventually no longer access. And that hurts.

Evolutionarily, human beings like comfort and need to save energy to have it. We store several things in our heads to release them every day when faced with tasks, challenges, and questions. If we don't have these savings, the effort is enormous, and a huge expense of energy. Therefore, changing is tiring. And that's why we adore the status quo.

We then find everyone in a state of exhaustion. Why is that?

Because we have never faced so many changes at the same time, in increasingly shorter cycles. We have never used so much energy.

And where is our refuge?

Two movements respond in part to this: conservatism and nostalgia. They are spread throughout our behaviors and respond to our need to save energy to survive. We can notice them on several fronts in our society. In daily articles, in our denial of technological advances, in the new versions that plague the entertainment world and that bring our souls some warmth, in the resurrection of past fashion trends, and so on...

This way we feel like we can use our stored resources, using less energy and living more moments in comfort.

I was going through the process of questioning my permanence at a company where I had worked for 22 years, in different roles and positions. Five years before I left, I joined a mentoring startup for middle and senior management executives. It was the beginning of a phase in which I was looking to broaden my horizons. It was also a small investment in a pool of startups, to learn about this new business ecosystem.

The most difficult question to answer was: "What would I like to do?"

And the only answer I had was the intention of not staying in the same area while exploring other sectors and work models.

By the time I left, I already had a routine with my mentoring and monthly meetings with the startup investor group. A blank screen appeared in front of me so that my action plan for a new period of life could be established.

Connections

At 53 years old, with 31 years of uninterrupted executive experience, with the intention of changing industries, how do you take the first step?

Firstly, I chose to deepen my self-discovery journey. More therapy, two mentors, books, and more time dedicated to my spirituality. Little by little, we clear our minds and converge onto a path. Throughout my life, what made the most sense to me weren't the most obvious choices. And this was reiterated to me then by my desire to do something new.

From media and entertainment, I formally studied agribusiness in an MBA program. At the same time, I went to Silicon Valley to learn about and participate in a conference that brings together universities, venture capital, and entrepreneurs. I trained myself for business advice. I took on a consultancy for a Latin American country, I made an agenda with big names of people full of wisdom, to exchange ideas and experiences. I talked to headhunters, analyzed proposals, and informally studied social psychology, and, thus, a year and three months have passed.

It's not simple. These movements often seemed scattered and required great energy, humility, and discipline to be around people, schedule conversations, and establish a mature and productive day, even if it was not clear what it was I wanted to do.

We need a lot of flexibility in our mental space to organize this. Up until then, everything came to me. I was in that system for some time, therefore, I exerted little effort and little expenditure of energy to get what I wanted.

I discovered that I didn't want to be an entrepreneur. I discovered that I didn't have the intention of facing a large company like the previous one I was at, and I wanted additions of new experiences, new topics, and new people who wanted to test out new work dynamics.

But that was my perspective. From there, I would need to put together a convincing, genuine, and truth-filled narrative, so that the market understood my set of knowledge and previous experiences. Another very important challenge.

That said, by conquering this new space, you will stir up all your comfort zones. All of them! From one second to another you go from being a reference to an apprentice, you need to use new words from your vocabulary and the way you operate is different. Besides all that, you need to meet new people–yes, this is the best part. But this requires a lot of openness and internal availability.

Today, I find myself in a role within a company whose proposal aims at the future and prosperity of the world, which has a tidy governance, deals with the largest companies operating in Brazil, which represents approximately 45% of the country's GDP, but is not one of them. In other words, I have the corporate world on my side, but I don't operate within it.

As I reflected on this year, I could feel a recent lesson I learned: "Imagination is more important than knowledge." I came across this phrase by Albert Einstein in a class about how to recover our imaginative capacity, where we were taught that the way we think about the future influences our actions in the present.

You need to dream, imagine, and then, act. This will give you a superpower you can't even imagine having. The superpower of transformation.

With the longevity revolution, we have all been invited to think about which paths we can follow if the current one stops being viable. Some have the privilege, like me, of taking a year to prepare and discover this new stage, but the vast majority may not have this chance.

Opportunity comes from where we least expect it. We need to go places we don't know, admire different subjects, talk to people of different origins and knowledge, and be open to this wave of newness. We need to learn to tame fear, as it will always be close by.

What is before us is an exponential world in constant change. And it will reach you faster and faster.

A friend I met recently, who moved from Brazil to Paris, said: "The first reinvention is brutal, but the others are much smoother." She's on her third.

Daniela Mignani worked at *Banco Nacional*, *Grupo Multiplan*, and *Grupo Globo* as General Director of non-sports paid channels. Currently, she is the director of institutional relations and communications at the *Brazilian Sustainable Development Business Council* (*CEBDS*). Daniela is also co-author of the book *Uma sobe e puxa a outra.*[6]

---

[6] Christiane Pelajo et al. (Org.), *Uma sobe e puxa a outra*, v. 2. São Paulo: Literare Books International, 2023. (Rise and Raise Others. – 2.ed. - WeBook Publishing, 2024.)

Adriana Alcântara

Connecting the dots

- Being able to adapt is an important differentiator and flexibility is a skill that helps a lot when it comes to creating connections and when we face adversity. First, we won't always meet people on our path with the same values, personalities, and profiles as ours. Flexibility is needed to find a way for these relationships to work. Second, what's not flexible breaks under pressure. By being flexible, we may be surprised at how much we can bear and how much further we can go.

- Human beings discover their flexibility when faced with difficulty, and can adapt – this can be for good (adaptability) or for evil (conformity).

- Helping someone implies flexibility: we need to give up something when we decide to extend a hand to another, and the same process happens when they help us.

- The opportunities that come our way are not always under ideal conditions. Flexibility at this time is fundamental to not letting these doors close.

Connections

And now it's your turn!

The time has come to strengthen your adaptability. This exercise is extremely easy and will help you train your mental and behavioral flexibility. Ready?

1. Select an activity you do with frequency, such as having breakfast, going to work, studying, or exercising.

2. Modify any significant detail in the way you accomplish this task. Here are some suggestions:

    - Going to work: if possible, choose a new route to commute or a different form of transport.
    - Studying: change the location where you usually study to something different, like a park, cafe, or even another location in your home.
    - Physical exercise: try a new form of movement you've never practiced.

3. After performing the modified task, reflect:

    - What was the experience of changing your routine like?
    - Did you feel uncomfortable? If yes, how did you deal with it?
    - What did this change teach you about your ability to adapt?

CHAPTER 5
Emotional Intelligence

Two words that do not seem to connect. Mainly because 'intelligence' refers to our rational side. Based on my personal and professional experiences, mixing this presumed paradox between the rational and the emotional is one of the biggest challenges and lessons in life. We are used to believing that emotional intelligence comes with time, after all, that pride and certainty of the youth make room for serenity. Which provides us a broader perspective of things. I particularly believe that time can indeed help us. Because the more we live, the more we make mistakes and, bit by bit, we progress. As that little flame inside of us that is ignited by our reaction to whatever bothers us reduces, emotional intelligence is still a skill that needs to be practiced every day. The positive side is: while living in a society and being part of a corporation, there's plenty of opportunities for that.

I would love to say that this is an ability I have mastered. However, that is far from the truth. The best I can do is tell you it is better than it was in the past. And that is a victory itself. I am an Aries sun with a Gemini rising. To whoever believes in Astrology, that says a lot. In many moments of my life, I have seen myself in the explosive combination of emotional foolishness and impulsivity. My strength and agility are good skills, but most of the time, I end up doing or saying something without any filter–the combination of an Aries brain with a Gemini big mouth–and I have to deal with the consequences later. Emotional Intelligence is deeply connected with being able to reflect. Reflecting takes time, which directly conflicts with my impulsive way of acting and speaking.

Connections

Nickelodeon time

I know I have said it before, but one of my major career privileges was the opportunity to work with extraordinary people. They elevated me in so many ways and they probably have no idea of. But, that does not mean I did not have my fair share of unpleasant people and situations. In those kinds of relationships, the magic combination of intelligence + emotions comes in handy. If I only knew that back in 2003...as we say in Brazil: we live, we learn, right?

After years working there and a certain familiarity with the company, I felt more comfortable about the problems I could identify. One of them was the outsourcing of professionals for management. In *Nickelodeon*'s national production, the entire production team was from a third party company that provided services to us. Since opening direct positions in these larger companies is always a challenge, the solution was outsourcing until the project grew and those internal positions could get approved.

It was a large team made of young people, because the dynamics of TV production in Brazil at the time sought a low cost-benefit ratio, in which everyone worked more than they should and earned less than they deserved– at least in my opinion.

When I openly expressed my opinions about the need to correct this practice, because of possible vulnerabilities to lawsuits, I opened a battlefront against another manager with whom I shared the channel's production management. At least, on paper. In reality, I also needed to go beyond my obligations to make things work. I could use many adjectives to describe this individual, but to avoid headaches, I will share a quick episode that involved him. I will leave the rest of the work to the reader's imagination.

One day, he disappeared for three days. No one could contact him, and he wouldn't answer or return calls. We were seriously concerned that something serious had happened. Then he arrived at the office with one of his legs immobilized with a boot race. When he returned, he told a story about being run over, being knocked unconscious, and breaking one of his feet. Deep down, everyone thought the story was strange, especially since it wasn't the first time he had disappeared like that. Every time he returned, there would be some reason or another, like a "my dog ate my homework" type of story. Still, no one said anything. The weekend came and on the following Monday, he showed up with the boot on his other leg.

That's right.

It could have been a scene from *The Office*, but it was our reality. We were working alongside a guy with a total lack of awareness, commitment, and professionalism. The worst part was that most of my work depended on his deliveries. A person who disappeared, showed up limping on one leg and days later was limping on the other. The possibility of not being able to do my job because someone else wasn't doing theirs was enough to make this Aries Ram lower her head, stomp on the floor, and prepare for the attack.

In all the places I've worked, before and after *Nick*, I've always delivered a lot more than expected. I believe I set very high standards for myself. I'm demanding. I like to learn and grow. The more I evolve, the more energy I have to keep evolving. I can't say for sure if this has always been my thing, or if I ended up developing this characteristic early in my career because of a perception, perhaps mistakenly made of what *exactly* was expected of me. A producer's job description is basically "solve everything." And there's always a lot to be solved.

In ballet, an art that seeks a perfection that does not exist, the teachers always put the best ballerinas at the front. Not only because the audience's focus will be on them, but also because the back rows can copy their movements. Guess where I insisted on being?

The funny thing is that, in theory, ballet came naturally to me. I was born with legs that are arched for dancing, the kind that ballerinas dream of and work hard to have. I also always heard that I had beautiful feet and that I would stand out because of them. It turns out that those who are born with these "ballerina feet" also have very fragile ankles, which require much more strengthening exercises than other people would need. It's like receiving a gift, but in order to actually use it and deserve it, you have to put in a lot more effort and train much harder. Otherwise, all I would have to show for would be a beautiful foot that came that way "from the factory" but weak and without the ability to do more elaborate steps.

Connections

Ballet was never just fun for me. It was a responsibility. For many years, I spent more than four hours per day dancing. I think I took to heart the idea that you only earn what you have if you work hard. And that has stuck with me throughout my life. Likewise, I have always believed in the slogan "No pain, no gain." During that time on *Nickelodeon*, the pain was watching my colleague dragging his feet and slouching. It was not easy to sit still.

When I looked around at my coworker, I didn't see what I valued most: dedication and gratitude for being there. If he needed help, I would certainly be available. I know that preparation comes from external situations and possibilities. However, dedication is something intrinsic to a person, having it or not is an entirely individual choice. For me, truly dedicating yourself to your professional life is already half the battle. This dedication can be demonstrated in many ways. For example by asking frequent questions or requesting feedback (i.e."What could I do better?"). But sometimes, dedication comes from a sparkle in the eye, from gratitude for simply having that opportunity in hand. It's up to the leader to see this and offer support.

I quietly put up with a lot of things and tried to have several open conversations about how we could grow together and do a better job. Although the exchanges seemed to flow, on a daily basis it was a festival of absences in meetings, with the team being demoralized by their behavior and the TV hosts complaining with reason. Not to mention the totally inappropriate actions and speeches, which today would result in big harassment lawsuits. Like, demanding that a very pregnant assistant director recorded all day under the hot sun or asking a ten-year-old host to eat a raw egg in front of the cameras.

A tragicomic part of this situation was the underage hosts. In order for a minor to work as an actor/TV host, a special license is required, as well as implementing a series of rules that aim to respect their education, mental and physical health, and their safety. Among these requirements, the law demands a responsible adult to be present in the studio– usually the father, mother, or legal guardian. As the norm, it is not easy to deal with the parents of these young talents. The children sometimes seem to be more mature than their parents. The adults are usually the ones who ask for special meals, complain about the costumes, are responsible for delays, etc. But when my management colleague was involved, the entire team thanked the heavens for the presence of the parents because this filtered out the atrocities and offered extra security to the minors. It would stop the guy from additional absurdities. Sometimes, it was still not enough.

One day, I got tired and started to inform the higher ups. They were located in Miami and weren't aware of this nonsense. At first, I was lighthearted, with a hint here and there, but since nothing changed–on the contrary, the nonsense only increased, so I started to be more assertive. I explained in no uncertain terms the additional effort I had to make outside of my own responsibilities because my colleague didn't dedicate himself. Many times, other people in the office would complain about his behavior, and I would make sure that somehow this complaint reached the leadership with all the details.

And that's when emotional intelligence comes into the equation. Even though I wasn't wrong in my arguments, I ended up putting myself in a position that wasn't right. In the search for a solution, I ended up becoming part of the problem. Exposing my view on the adversities involving another professional so openly left me politically fragile within the company. From the corporate perspective, I had no right to expose the facts in that way. To be honest, I also didn't try to understand why he was behaving that way. Maybe I could have helped, but I wasn't thinking that way.

When the situation was becoming unsustainable, our respective bosses called us to a process alignment meeting. The alignment was of our relationship in order to understand the boundaries of each person's roles and responsibilities. Because at that moment, the impression was that there was someone who was not working, and another who was only criticizing. In this view, both executives were wrong.

The relationship was already impossible, so they booked us on separate flights to Miami. When I was already on the plane, cell phone turned off, seatbelts fastened, and swiping through the catalog of movies available to keep me entertained for the next eight hours, I heard the unmistakable voice of a flight attendant saying my name over the system, summoning me to the cabin. There, I was informed that they had received a message telling me to disembark from the aircraft, as my boss in Miami had

Connections

called to say that I was supposed to get off the plane. It's not every day that a situation like this happens, and worried that something bad might have happened, I got off the plane and called her. Completely embarrassed, my boss told me that my colleague had said that he was not psychologically fit to travel.

I went all the way back through customs, thinking about how insane it was to wait until the last minute to say he wouldn't be traveling–in itself, was enough to validate my complaints about him. It only takes a few seconds to see the amount of trouble he was willing to cause to several people: (1) the disrespect for the company after having bought two tickets, organized hotels, and arranged meeting schedules, (2) the disrespect towards me, because it's always fun and easy to go back and forth at an International airport like Guarulhos, right? (3) the disrespect for the rest of the world, especially the two bosses, who had worked incredibly hard to get in touch with the airline, locate me on the plane, and prevent it from taking off–of all the other passengers who got their trip delayed. There is a decent amount of bureaucracy involved in canceling someone who already boarded to leave the plane, especially if they were going to the United States after 9/11. Not to mention that I still had to find my suitcase and remove it from the plane. Just as I imagine that he must have, to some degree, disturbed the control tower with that unnecessary nonsense.

I wanted to tell my boss all this as well as the entire airport, maybe even the entire world. I was furious, but I kept quiet. I believed that the absurdity of it all spoke for itself, and the given justification alone deserved a deeper evaluation of his performance and conduct in everyday life, especially when dealing with children. However, that was the end of the story. We never had our meeting with the bosses. I think after the episode on the flight to Miami. It became clear that no amount of mediation would have enough impact to fix the way things were going. We felt like two kindergarteners who couldn't behave and now had to have a talk with their aunts–but at least I was going to confront him with other adults who could do something about it. But no, not even that occasion served to demonstrate who I had to deal with every day. The lack of commitment and professionalism only served to make my blood boil even more because I continued to have to do my job and everything he failed to do, in addition to

Adriana Alcântara

balancing the mood. When I thought I had seen it all...another crazy thing came along.

At one point, we received a letter that basically gave us thirty days to resolve our issues, make the processes work, and get things back on track. It turns out that there was nothing to "adjust" on my part. I wasn't the one who broke one leg and put the cast on the other one, nor who called during the flight to say I wasn't fit to board, or who didn't show up for meetings. I was so clear that I was being the professional in the story of what I should and shouldn't do. All I could do was keep doing my job and wait. Even so, I took the initiative and went to talk to him. I asked him what was wrong and what I could do better. He shut off and simply said that everything was fine. The thirty days were up, and guess what happened? I was fired.

Because of all these Kafkaesque circumstances (I'm glad I was able to use this word in my book!), I ended up giving myself the right to behave a little politically incorrectly. But that "little" was enough for me to be dismissed when it came time to weigh in. We all knew that he was protected by his boss. How else could he have stayed there for so long if he wasn't a brilliant guy whose deliverables overcame the problems he created? What we didn't know–or at least I didn't know–was that the strength of his boss' internal politics was greater than mine, and when the rope snapped, the shorter end was on my side.

I have had a long career and have seen a lot of things happen, but the insanity that surrounded this period of my professional life was unique. After almost two years, he was finally fired for very serious reasons I would rather not discuss. But at that time, several labor lawsuits involving production staff and hosts had already fallen on *Nickelodeon*'s lap–the same ones that I warned so much about.

With more gray hairs to show for my experience, I believe that if I had had more emotional intelligence I would have been able to navigate this situation better. How? By filtering out the snakes and lizards around me better. And even by letting that man harm himself alone until he lost his job– instead of repeating everything that was wrong. Who knows, paradoxically, if I hadn't spoken so much I would have been heard, and the whole thing would have had a different outcome. I don't recommend staying quiet in any way and not speaking up in situations like this, but the balance is quite delicate. There is content and form, and both have to be at the right volume. I wasn't wrong in the fact, but my certainty of being right and the degree of surrealism of the situations made me speak too loudly, and in the wrong way. The lack of emotional intelligence clouded my ability to read the room. This reading is often the key. Unfortunately, this wasn't the time that I would learn my lesson.

Life demands our emotional intelligence until we learn the lesson

It was 2012 and my maternity leave was in the end when an executive consultant called me to say they were interested in talking about a confidential position. My daughter, Maria Victória, was born in Rio de Janeiro, and I had the privilege of having six months of paid leave. When I was about to return to work, due to a restructuring at *Oi*, I was given three more months at home. I was unsure whether I would have a job or not, but it was some extra time to spend with my daughter. During this period, a lot had happened at *Oi*. A large part of my team was no longer there and I was not sure myself if I wanted to go back. So, I accepted the invitation to participate in the process of a secret company, and in the final phase, I discovered that it was *Apple*. I received the offer on the condition that I move to São Paulo, so I returned to my hometown with two Cariocas in my luggage: my husband Renato Tocantins and my daughter Vicky. Since my husband was already in the oil and gas industry and had important meetings in the Rio-São Paulo axis, we were able, or almost able, to accommodate everyone's dynamics.

Apple was about to launch iTunes in Latin America and organized their directors under three pillars: music, apps and movies, each with a leader. I was responsible for movies and everyone reporting to Christopher Moser, leader of Latin America.

When Christopher went to Rio to formalize the proposal, he said he would like me to go with him to São Paulo before I actually started, so I could introduce myself internally. Of course, I accepted. I was excited to go back to work, and although I had never owned anything from *Apple*, I had always admired the brand. To give you an idea, I handed over my corporate cell phone when I left *Oi*, which was a BlackBerry, the leader during that time, and got a prepaid device so cheap that it looked like a toy. Even so, I went to São Paulo.

In the middle of a meeting, the phone started ringing inside my bag, and from the sound of it, anyone could tell it was a very simple phone. I pretended it wasn't me. I sweated, ignored my bag, and put it under the table. The phone kept ringing until Christopher told me I had better answer it. I took it out of my bag, wanting to hide inside of it. Everyone at the table stared at the phone in disbelief that the new *Apple* executive was using that device. It was my husband calling, worried and wanting to know if I had arrived safely in São Paulo. That was my start at one of the most admired companies in the world. Once again, emotional intelligence would have come in handy because I could have used my wits to manage that embarrassment.

iTunes already existed in Mexico, but it was managed by the United States. The idea was to launch it in other Latin American countries, including Brazil, where a large part of the team would be based and transfer the management of Mexico to that team while focusing on growth. In this mixed bag of structures, the team became responsible for operations in Latin America, Spain, and Portugal. After all, all these countries speak Spanish and Portuguese, right? And we reported to Christopher, who was based in Madrid.

My main responsibility was to get independent distributors to put their films on *iTunes*, remembering that no one knew about Transactional Video on Demand (TVOD) and much less its business model. They also didn't understand that Apple didn't share any projection and wanted non-exclusive rights to the films in exchange for a percentage of the revenue, which without projection meant nothing.

Performing this work in Brazil was a challenge. My professional connections were in the TV world, not in the filming world. So, I had to build everything from scratch, including a new house in São Paulo, since my husband and I decided to keep a structure in Rio due to his work. Little by little, I navigated and established new connections. In the bigger studios, the rights for TV and DVD were managed by the digital teams that took care of

Connections

DVD. Which meant that small divisions were not priorities. This process happened to a lesser extent in Mexico, since *iTunes* already existed there, but still, many independents were not yet signed, and the catalog needed to grow.

We expanded the launch of *iTunes* store to other Spanish-speaking Latin American countries. There were many trips to meet partners at *Apple* events, and the combination of everything meant I spent about twenty days a month flying or staying in a hotel away from my baby, who was just over a year old. It was very common for me to wake up at night to go to the bathroom without immediately remembering where I was. I would arrive at breakfast and not know which language to speak. With this routine–or lack thereof–I was unable to eat properly or exercise, and every time I heard the word "trip" I would start to get tachycardia. At the time I didn't recognize it, but I was having recurring anxiety attacks and there was no sign of any change in the dynamics of my work on the horizon.

After a year, Christopher accepted the position of head of *iTunes* in Europe and moved to London. As a result, the director of applications for Latin America took his place, based in Brazil, and a new executive was brought in to take charge of his old area–and all this changing of roles ended up triggering one of the most difficult moments of my professional life, as it quickly overflowed, compromising my health.

Everybody, including the newcomer, were my peers. When he was promoted, the application director had as much management experience as any of us. For a long time, I thought it was odd that the company had decided not to bring in an outsider to lead the company but to instead promote someone from within. In my view, none of us were ready to sit in Christopher's chair. But, I decided to keep my thoughts to myself

In addition to the work on the content that would be made available by iTunes, which already involved very close contact with government agencies, there was an extremely important knot to be untied: *Apple* wanted to operate *iTunes* in Brazil in *Reais*, otherwise the product could be unviable in the country, initially due to the perception that it would become very expensive due to international transaction fees and the disparity between the Dollar and the Real. Furthermore, they also anticipated a future tax problem, in parallel with the challenge of operating formally in Brazil–without prices in Dollars, and without being limited to those with international credit cards, which greatly limits the potential customer base. This type of operation is called "bringing the company onshore."

At that time, there were still a lot of discussions about the Condecine tax to streaming services (like *Netflix* and *iTunes*) in order to protect the visibility of the national productions. Regulated by *Ancine*, the *National Cinema Agency*, which now requires that all cable TV networks have a minimum quota for national production on primetime. The idea was to follow the same concept with the streaming services. The challenge was the fact that they had an immense amount of international content, from countries all over the world, and Brazil did not have the same amount to make up even a fraction of that scene.

To find a way to meet halfway there, I would participate in that dynamic, because almost no one from the government that was participating in the negotiations table spoke fluent English, and *Apple* did not have anyone else, on the executive level, who spoke Portuguese, besides me. That also implicated another perception matter. We were already looking for an opportunity to become an exception to the Brazilian rules, and the first yet most anticipated question from the government side: "With such a music industry here, so many qualified people in the market, why is the person from iTunes that is in charge of the discussions in Brazil a foreigner on a temporary work visa? The starter pistol was fired only to shoot us on the foot. And just like that, the task was mine. I have always participated in the meetings to at least give the impression that it wasn't a complete international operation, but in the face of such a fragile structure, I became the reference to the government during the conversations among *Apple*.

So, besides managing the relations with Brazilian sectors and agencies due to video content, I was given a non-official and non-requested leadership position, important for the success of *Apple*'s venture in Brazil. Bottom line, I did not spend that much time thinking about it. The only thing that mattered to me was to execute my job well but here is when the first dark clouds started to form in what would become a perfect storm.

What I learned, and keep learning, is that the problem created by the lack of emotional intelligence only gets traction if there's no resistance on the other side. As they say: it takes two to tango. No matter the circumstances that put me in a spot where I should not necessarily be, the lack of maturity or emotional intelligence of my new boss made him seem less powerful, or his voice to be less heard, or whatever else, creating an uncomfortable atmosphere. That wasn't a risk, because even if I had a professional background to take on a bigger challenge than the one I already had, I was miles away from being able to take over what I already had, mainly due to my personal situation.

First of all, I was the only woman and Brazilian on this team. The other three were Colombians who already knew each other and had strong connections. Because I had just had a kid, the only thing that mattered to me outside the office was my family, my daughter. I mean, my interaction with them outside the office was zero. They all went out together, extended their trips to enjoy weekends in London, Miami, Madrid, and even Buenos Ayres. The lack of time–and honestly desire–did not leave room to build a relationship with them, something that used to be my personal trademark. Only years later I realized that we all lived in the same neighborhood and I had never invited any of them to my house, something I always loved to do. No one from *Apple* ever came to my house, and when I think about that, it flabbergasted me. How haven't I ever noticed this weird dynamic that was happening inside my mind?

Could I have done that? Not only could I have, but now I understand that I should have done it. Would that have been a political move more than a desire? Yes, but maybe a small gesture like that could have put down some walls and shown them that I was part of that group. Of course I was living that personal moment with complete lack of energy to high-executive politics from a giant company such as *Apple*. With such a Herculean job on my hands and a small child at home, I was stretching myself too thin. At that time, that was all I could see and care about. I did not notice that that was exactly what was distancing more and more from that group, whose context strengthened the bonds between the other members. I didn't need to become best friends with them, but perhaps these attitudes would have helped our relationships.

I questioned if my resistance was because I thought I should be the one chosen for the promotion and concluded, to my relief, that I shouldn't. After all, I had no chance of doing anything beyond what was already in front of me. After all, I truly believed that none of us were capable of moving up a step in the hierarchy at that moment, but it wasn't up to me to think anything of it. My initial feeling was that the right thing to do would have been to bring in a leader from somewhere else, but who knows. Maybe they tried and failed. Or maybe I was in the wrong place, since I expected to have someone with a different profile as my boss, someone I could admire and learn more from. In any case, no matter what was the reason for not developing a better relationship with that group, the truth is that I didn't reduce my professional commitment at all. However, the cost started to become too high. I started to have phobias of flying and panic attacks in different places around the world. The attacks increased in frequency and duration. My whole body would hurt. I don't know if it was because of the lack of an exercise routine, the poor diet, or if my emotional state was so weak that it started to hurt physically as a form of alarm. Regardless, I didn't listen.

I kept following the same path, after all, what could happen? The answer: a living hell. In this dynamic I traveled more and more, lost more weight, had more tachycardia, and more panic attacks. Things were not going well.

The only time I wanted to be away from home and away from my daughter was when I was in the office. Anything longer than that was too much time for me. But since that was part of my job, what I tried to do was optimize it as much as possible: if the meeting was on Monday in Miami, I would travel on Sunday morning and go straight to the Apple office. If the trip required more days of meetings, the minute after they ended, I would head to the airport. Even then, I was always on the plane, and it was a complicated issue, even more so with the episodes. I will share a loose summary of what the conversations in the office with my new boss were like:

"Listen, it's been three weeks since you've been to Mexico, right? It would be good to go back next week."

"But have you done anything there yet? Do you have anything to solve?"

"No, but it would be good to go."

Connections

So, I would travel nine hours to Mexico to hear the same thing from the same people: no, nothing had happened and there was nothing to be resolved. I would come back from Mexico and feel relieved because I wouldn't have to repeat that waste of time and money for a few more weeks.

"Listen, I'm going to Madrid. I think it's a good idea for us all to go together to catch up and blah blah blah…"

"But I just got back from Mexico."

"I understand, but you haven't seen your partners in Spain for a month."

We weren't in the era of online meetings yet, but Skype already existed and everything could be handled that way. But no, I had to put myself on a plane unnecessarily. As a result, my emotional and physical fragility only got worse and things continued to go downhill. My health was increasingly affected, crises were more frequent, and as a result, my deliveries began to be affected by health issues.

A lot of things went through my head at that time. Why can't men understand the impact of motherhood? Why do they end up seeing it as a weakness that will make a female employee perform less than a male employee? Why do some men have difficulty dealing with a dedicated woman who works and has a career? Why does this bother them so much?

In reality, I believe that these questions are answered by the lack of emotional intelligence. This lack leads us all to insecurity, which by itself leads us to use all sorts of tricks to stand out positively. It is easier to keep women in the background when it comes to a promotion, or a situation that will give them greater visibility, putting family and motherhood on the table, for example. It is like betting on a race where the men come out halfway ahead, you know?

I was fading away, and while this was happening, I felt like my boss was coming up with ideas to make my life a living hell. *Apple*'s policy wasn't just about firing someone. It was necessary to justify, and very well, the reason why that person was being dismissed from the company, especially when that person was delivering results. But I had my weak points: international travel and now my mental and physical health. For me, it was no longer possible, and I knew I had to leave.

Adriana Alcântara

That's when Egon Zehnder contacted me. In 2001, I had been nominated by then president of *Google* Brazil, Fábio Coelho, for a position leading *YouTube* in Brazil, but I was about to give birth. I did the first interview and shared my personal situation, declining the position believing that it wasn't exactly the right time to take on such a challenge. Although, I was very happy with the consideration and delighted with the opportunity.

In 2013, Egon Zehnder considered me for a position at *Twitter*, and I was desperate to leave Apple. I went through the entire process with great dedication. I wasn't a *Twitter* user, but I still worked hard and made it organically part of my body, as someone from Generation Z. I made it to the final round and Twitter flew the two finalists to the final interview in San Francisco. I packed my bags and made up a lame excuse to travel. I did the interview and gave it my all, but unfortunately, they chose the other candidate.

When Luis Giolo from Egon Zehnder called me to give me the news, I broke down. I was devastated. And I still don't know if it was because I really wanted that job or if I was desperate to have a noble excuse to get out of the nightmare that was my life at *Apple*. In the end, I learned valuable lessons that I would carry with me for the next challenges. If I had had emotional intelligence at the time, it would have been easier, but we learn through our mistakes.

Emotional Intelligence

Carolina Andrade

Almost fifteen years ago, my path crossed with Adri's when I could no longer handle the trouble I had gotten myself into by naively crossing the line between personal and professional life. In search of a new beginning, I met her while trying to guess the answer to the question: "Is your profile more generalist or do you pay more attention to details?" I wasn't the first option in the process, but my odds played in our favor: the chosen candidate hadn't accepted the offer, and I didn't feel ready to move to another city

Connections

either. I stayed in Rio with Dri as a manager at a company where I spent a short time chronologically, but a long period of learning.

Shortly after, different companies took us to São Paulo and we crossed paths again– this time, not as collaborators, but as friends. I had no one in the city and happily accepted invitations for pizzas, which nourished me emotionally. And while Adri traveled to *Apple*, I tried to reciprocate her friendship by playing with an adorable baby who taught me how motherhood would be an inevitable path for me.

I have to confess that when I received the invitation to contribute to this chapter, I was both flattered and surprised: after all, what qualifies me to expand the conversation about emotional intelligence? Adri and I share the same nonconformity of self-development that pushes us one step forward every day–perhaps that is where our mutual professional admiration comes from. But balancing daily emotions is also a challenge for both of us. So, I decided to move away from theoretical pretensions and share what I have learned over the years balancing my professional and academic life and the pains and pleasures that raising three children presents me with every day.

In my experience, emotional intelligence is finding the balance between resilience and self-care. It is being aware of what personal development, situational challenges, and other people's responsibilities are. It is knowing how to move through life taking on the appropriate amount of self-accountability, without failing to give back what is due to others. And for me, communication is at the heart of this game because it is what allows us to work through our challenges, but also engage those who need to overcome their own in the constant search for personal growth.

I didn't always have this perception. When excesses were openly committed, it was easy to draw the line between what was acceptable or not. Of course, communicating this boundary always brought challenges, especially in unequal power relationships. But when a boss uses a "dog whistle" to summon the team–especially the younger employees–the insanity of the situation clearly empowers the victims. In times of #MeToo, it is almost unthinkable that something like this would happen again without attracting the attention of compliance. But what about when these abuses are subtle and endorsed by a corporate culture that does not punish them and, in many cases, even encourages them?

During some of the years of my professional life, I was torn between my visceral dedication to what I did and the suffering of having coworkers–and in some cases, even friends–actively engaged in creating a toxic environment to win a zero-sum game. As a reward, I was participating in a lavish project that I had the privilege to lead after much mistaken exposure (you may see the glamour, but you don't see the mess in the back). And as a pivot, I was a leader who noticed what was happening but chose not to take a stand while hoping that time would make it magic. Jokes, indirect remarks and small rudeness alternated with aggressive narratives, to the point that I began to doubt myself. It was all so intense that sometimes I thought I really deserved that treatment.

It was with the help of other women that made me realize the unfair position that game was trying to push me into. And what seemed like a fight between good and evil began to take on more complex contours. The project was successful, the opposition lost strength, and the newly gained political capital empowered me to be less resilient and more vocal. When I look back, I see that I spent too much time trying to justify myself instead of improving myself in the political tango that is almost always necessary in corporate life. It was by changing my narrative that the score began to move in favor of my team. As the philosopher Wittgenstein would conclude, "The limits of my language were the limits of my world."[7]

Between therapy and my master's degree, I decided to pursue an academic career to strengthen myself, and I delved deeper into the analysis of communication strategies that try to stop us without saying it openly. There are fascinating studies that help us understand the subject from different perspectives. I will mention two, and I hope they generate as many reflections for you as the countless debates I engaged in after learning about them.

In 2012, *Google* set themselves out to understand the components that affect team performance. The leaders of *Project Aristotle*–made up of sociologists, psychologists, statisticians and engineers–monitored the dynamics of approximately two hundred teams, both high- and low-

---

[7] Wittgenstein: 'Os limites da minha linguagem são os limites do meu mundo'. *Superinteressante*, 29 out. 2015. Disponível em: <https://super.abril.com.br/ideias/ os-limites-da-minha-linguagem-sao-os-limites-do-meu-mundo-wittgenstein>. Acesso em: 22 set. 2024.

performing, in search of patterns. By comparing empirical experience with the available literature on group norms, the researchers concluded that psychological safety is the factor with the greatest impact on delivery.

The Massachusetts Institute of Technology (MIT) was able to define the concept of psychological safety by studying the interaction between around seven hundred people divided into groups with a series of tasks to complete. Two patterns were always present in those with the best performance: equal speaking time and empathy between team members. The participants of one of the groups could present above-average intelligence individually, but it was the prioritization of standards, which increased collective intelligence, that actually made the difference in performance. Aristotle, in his work *Metaphysics*, was correct in stating that the whole transcends the mere sum of its parts, indicating the existence of an essence that unites and enhances the individual elements.[8]

"The Aristotle Project is a reminder that when companies try to optimize everything, it can become easy to forget that success is often built on experiences that can't be optimized," concluded journalist Charles Duhigg in an article for the *New York Times*. "That's the case for emotional interactions and complicated conversations or discussions about who we want to be and how our teammates make us feel".[9]

The second study focuses on our word choices. For Lakoff and Johnson, metaphor is embedded in everyday life, both in thought and action. And one of the most eloquent examples is the metaphor "argument is war." The authors offer several examples that demonstrate how much this concept permeates our positioning in a debate. "His arguments are indefensible," "he attacked every weak point in my argument and I have never won a discussion with him," are some of the ways in which this worldview is represented by language.

---

[8] Aristóteles. *Metafísica*. Trad. Edson Bini. São Paulo: Edipro, 2012. Livro viii.
[9] Duhigg, Charles. "What Google learned from its quest to build the perfect team". *The New York Times*. Disponível em: <https://www.nytimes. com/2016/02/28/magazine/what-google-learned-from-its-quest-to-build-the- perfect-team.html>. Acesso em: 15 set. 2024.

"The essence of metaphor is to understand and experience one thing in terms of another," explain the linguists, who challenge: "What if we experienced a debate as a dance, rather than as a war?"[10]

In the age of artificial intelligence, emotional intelligence remains relevant among the most important skills for today's professionals, according to the World Economic Forum.[11] The idea that we can have healthier and more collaborative interactions has been guiding research in different areas around the world. This search involves the development of more humane corporate cultures, but also the individual awareness that we take part in this construction every day. We need to position ourselves not in order to win a battle, but to contribute to a debate. We need to raise our voices not to defend ourselves but to ensure that they are heard. We need to talk about what we are feeling in order to find a meaning that allows us to grow collectively. Let's talk about it?

Carolina Andrade Dombrasas has worked for about twenty years in content curation, distribution, and marketing. Having worked for Viacom Brasil, Grupo Globo and Google, her experience with international teams sparked her curiosity about the role of different organizational cultures in stimulating or inhibiting debate in large companies. With a degree in journalism, she is currently a PhD candidate in applied linguistics and language studies, studying how communication can build bridges in times of such polarization.

---

[10] Lakoff, George; joHNsoN, Mark. *Metáforas da vida cotidiana*. Campinas: Mercado de Letras, 2002.
[11] World Economic Forum, "The Future of Jobs Report 2020". out. 2020. Disponível em: <https://www3.weforum.org/docs/WEF_Future_of_Jobs_2020.pdf>. Acesso em: 22 set. 2024.

Connecting the dots

- Nothing is above our health. At the slightest sign that you are not doing well, stop, think, and then redirect the course of your walk. Running on a road that is not working will only make you hurt yourself.

- Don't expect from others the greatness to put themselves in your shoes and understand your pain and your situation. Many people only evaluate the volume of your work delivery at any cost, as if we were machines and not human beings. But despite the fact that most people are like this, there are exceptions, and I insist on being one.

- You are not worth more or less despite the company you work for. You have your value, and you will always have it wherever you are or aren't. I should have left Apple much earlier and not waited for a new opportunity. I spent months hurting myself when I already knew that my future was not there, but it took a lot of courage to leave a position of trust at one of the most admired companies in the world.

- As a manager, never forget to learn as much as you can about the lives of the people on your team outside of work. They are humans and have emotions, personal difficulties, and challenges. All of this comes and goes with them even at work. Try to be empathetic, kind, understanding, and helpful.

- Even though the passing of the years can diminish the flame of our reaction to discomfort, emotional intelligence is a skill that needs to be worked on every day.

- A problem generated by the absence of emotional intelligence only gains traction if it does not encounter resistance from the other side – something close to the popular wisdom that states that when one person does not want to, two people will not fight.

- Emotional intelligence is finding the balance between resilience and self-care. It is being aware of what personal development, situational challenge and other people's responsibility are.

Now it's your turn!

We have seen in this chapter that working on emotional intelligence is something we need to do continuously and that, although we are not always able to react to situations in the best possible way, we can learn from our mistakes. Use the space below to reflect on the most recent event that threw you off track and write down how you acted and what the results/consequences were. Then write down how, thinking from a more distant perspective, you think you should have acted and what you believe the consequences would have been. Analyze why you did not act in the best way the first time and what you should remember to act in the best way next time.

Adriana Alcântara

CHAPTER 6
Listening

It is necessary to seek balance among all people to make the show happen. Within a group that needs to move in the same direction, it would be useless for one person to stand out and not the others. What matters is team harmony. That is what leads to the best results. I like to compare it to ballet. During rehearsals, each dancer individually gives their best, lifts their leg as high as they can, and holds it until they can no longer do it. On stage, in front of an audience, what matters is not the individual beauty, but rather, the group's ability to balance all the steps to appear as identical and harmonious as possible. This perfection only happens because all the performers dance with sharp eyes, observing the movements of the others and adapting to each other. In classes and rehearsals, each dancer gives their best to improve individually, but at the time of a performance, the dynamic is different.

During the presentation, some dancers who could do four or more pirouettes do only three to match everyone else and get the best result for the group. Ballet has its solo moments, where only one dancer stands out and gives his or her best, but when the whole group is dancing, what counts is the best that everyone can do together! It's a playful way of showing the famous saying: "The whole is greater than the sum of its parts."

After leaving *Apple*, I was invited to join the *Food Network*. After working for a telecom company (*Oi*) and a technology company (*Apple*), I was back to my roots, cable TV. However, in addition to my first area of experience (production and programming), I would also be involved in other fields, such as marketing and digital strategy. This was another big challenge. In 2013, cable TV channels were already having difficulty growing given the arrival of Netflix in Brazil, which changed consumption

129

Connections

habits for movies, series, documentaries, etc. That year, although there was a lot of discussion between *Netflix* and internet service providers, which was essential for the service to work, it was a period of great growth for *Netflix*, and Brazil has always stood out as a priority market after the United States.

The invitation for this new challenge came from Marcio Fonseca, with whom I had sat at the negotiating table back when I was at *OiTV*, when he was responsible for distributing the *Fox* group channels. The most curious thing is that he sent me a message to meet for coffee, and I, in the rush of *Apple* travels, didn't get to schedule it and didn't imagine it would be a work invitation. But the message came in another way: Marcio had hired the production company Casablanca to handle the promotions and localizations of the international programming. Yes, the same one for which I did the commercials for Estrela toys when I was a child. In a conversation with Arlette Siaretta, he said that he really wanted to bring me, but that I was at *Apple*. He thought it would be impossible to convince me. Well, as we say in Brazil: "those who see face, don't see heart." That's when the stars aligned and Arlette said:

"But she's dying to get out of there. She's already told me that if I hear anything, I should bring her name up."

And so, I went on to lead the marketing, production, and digital areas, later expanding to negotiations with operators, where I scored the goal of placing the channel on *Claro/Net*, the largest cable TV base in Brazil at the time. Without being on Net, a channel didn't have the reach and relevance to sell commercials which limited the business' revenue to distribution alone and, therefore, the business plan wasn't sustainable.

Right after, Daniela Branco, who had been my student at FAAP in 2006, was returning from Barcelona and unhappy with the dynamics of the agency where she worked. We aligned the stars again, and I brought Daniela in to take care of marketing. I didn't know how to fry an egg, but I knew how to make TV and that was enough. With active listening, we put together a trustworthy team committed to doing the best.

We did a lot of cool things together. The local production was beautiful and had good visibility. We developed Brazilian programs to create a good mix with the programming that would be translated abroad. One of the programs, called *Na laje (At the Rooftop)*, featured recipes with Brazilian ingredients from all over, and each episode featured a guest band to play. In addition to promoting Brazil's culinary diversity, we also gave opportunities for small bands to showcase their work on television. Another program, called *Menu*, showed a culinary agenda, talking about interesting places and interviewing professionals from all the gastronomy spectrum. We interviewed famous chefs, but we also showed emerging baristas, unusual places, and street food.

Since the channel's marketing budget was minimal, the digital strategy had to be very strong to make up for the fat check we didn't have. But nothing was a problem because we were creative. We had licensed a program called *I Could Kill for Dessert*, hosted by Danielle Noce. She was writing a cookbook that would be released by *Melhoramentos*, and we thought: why not include the *Food Network* seal as a brand on the book? I had met *Melhoramentos* CEO Breno Lerner when I was at *Apple* and temporarily held meetings and closed negotiations for iTunes on the books front, while they searched for the executive who would run that part of the business. I made the call, scheduled the meeting, and half an hour later, we agreed to have the channel's logo on the cover of the book, making a connection between the products. At the launch session, the line stretched all the way down *Paulista Avenue*–and there we were, kind of hitchhiking while also adding value.

Another really cool project was a digital content focused on sustainability, in which the recipes were made with parts of food that we normally throw away. It was called *Restô* (a slang/joke about leftovers). With this project, we invaded the communication area of the São Paulo subway with an exhibition. Each poster had a QR code that led to the channel's website, where the video of the recipe was. Our partner in this endeavor was Juliana Alcides, who led the internal communication area at *ViaQuatro* and embraced our ideas with great affection. Juliana is a childhood friend of Luísa Fernandes, who I met at *Nickelodeon* and is my *comadre* (I'm her daughter's godmother and sister in life). The goal of her work was to inform the population about sustainability, safety, and culture, but not everyone remembers to offer ideas in such valuable spaces as the subway–often with a budget allocated to buy media, these free opportunities end up being left aside. While you can showcase your content as long as it

Connections

adds value to the community, there are limitations to how your brand can appear, so it takes creativity and time–something that people with big budgets don't always care about having.

Restô was so successful that we renewed it to a second season, called *Restô dontê* (following the theme of slang/jokes about leftovers), with recipes using foods that were no longer so fresh, like rice that had been in the fridge for four days and turned into pizza dough. We managed to get distribution and hired an advertising sales team.

Everything was going great until the *Food Network* was bought by *Discovery*, and when these corporate moves happen, there is always a risk involved. In the process of restructuring, layoffs happen. Many people started looking for other job openings, instead of waiting for the day when the merger would actually happen. If there is a job for you, great! Go for it. If not, you leave and get a bonus for staying and taking a risk.

Because I loved my job there, I was on the wait-and-see team when I got a call from a recruitment consultancy talking about a job opening at *Cartoon Network*. Since my time at *Nickelodeon*, I have come to admire *Cartoon Network* a lot. The truth is, however, that I saw this job as a step back from where I was in my career.

In the company structure at that time, that specific position was about production and programming, and I was already very involved in marketing and business. I understood that this was not for me, but the head of that position, Pablo Zuccarino called Celia Kakitani, who had previously worked with him and was now my colleague at the *Food Network*, asking about me and possible references. I don't know what Celinha said, but the result was that Pablo became obsessed about me.

I was on vacation in New York with my husband when Pablo sent me a message to schedule a phone call. I agreed, but I didn't prepare myself. I answered the call from the bathroom in our hotel room so I wouldn't wake Renato. During that call, I had several "brutally honest" moments. I said that I no longer believed in TV, that I thought that scheduled programming were numbered, etc. I said every single thing that could make Pablo forget me, but he only thought more and more that I was the perfect person for that position. Pablo listened to everything I had to say and even what I left between the lines.

"What do you think of linear TV?" he asked, using a term referring to the traditional broadcast television model.

"Well, for starters, TV is dead," I replied. "Everything is going digital, brands and content that don't understand strategy will die. The audience migrated a long time ago and TV companies don't want to recognize it and change their business model, so they'll end up getting run over. I've never done scheduled programming, there's always been someone extremely technical about it, so don't assume that I know schedule strategies."

In fact, I believed in what I was saying, but I spoke with such freedom that they were suicidal responses. But the funny thing is that the more I played against myself, the more he said, "That's all I want to hear." I don't recommend anyone to do this kind of reverse engineering for a job interview, but since it ended up working out, I decided to make my considerations in case, hypothetically, I got the job. I didn't want to be a person exclusively for content and programming. I wanted to be in charge of the channel as a whole. We had more conversations, these based on some presentations to discuss the future of the channel.

After a lot of back and forth, we finally came to an agreement and that's how I became the General Director of *Cartoon Network*, in theory the number one person on the channel in Brazil.

Listening is your greatest ally when it's time to get everyone to dance to the same tune

It's never easy to arrive at a new place and start writing a new chapter of history. Even with many miles traveled and advanced steps in my career, I still had butterflies in my stomach about how I would be received by the new team. But in the case of *Cartoon*, there was an additional apprehension, and I imagine this was mutual because of the restructuring plans–a word that every professional feels a chill on the back of their neck when they hear it, because, as I said before, it usually involves cuts.

At that time, a team was already in place, but since the company had a matrix structure in which the areas reported to several leaders, my presence would centralize things a little with a broader scope than that of the person who previously occupied the position. Large companies usually face this structural dilemma. I don't think either one is perfect. Both have their positive points and their major challenges. In a matrix structure, in which people from other countries report to the verticals of each area, there is much more optimization and the possibility of scaling the business with fewer people on the teams. However, this format means that the peculiarities of each country are left aside, and this harms the growth potential. In a horizontal structure, the localization of the strategy is prioritized and local opportunities are faster to execute, but it is more difficult to scale and optimize the external structure.

There was also the cherry on top. There is a reason why romantic relationships in the workplace are viewed with suspicion by companies, sometimes even being prohibited: when things go wrong on one side, they tend to spill over onto the other, and invariably spill over onto colleagues as well. So, I arrived at *Cartoon*, and in addition to a horrible atmosphere, I found out about a situation where two team members had recently ended their marriage. In an obvious fictional exaggeration, sometime later I started to joke that it was like a group of brilliant children together in a playground, who during the transition between my predecessor and me were left without adult supervision while eating ice cream for lunch and sleeping late. But the fact is that my arrival was an order shock to the house, and the path we followed from then on was one of the most fulfilling experiences I have ever had as a person and a professional, in a place that at first seemed to have nothing interesting to offer me. This was my first lesson from this experience: we must always keep an open mind because the paths to learning and fulfillment are not always obvious.

The most important thing was to reclaim our sense of where we were. That was *Cartoon Network*: an incredible channel and brand whose essence is love as marked by the history of different generations. It is an essential part of the growth of millions of people with followers of all ages and wonderful content to work on children's values.

Sure, everyone works for a salary that is deposited at the beginning of the month, but how incredible it is to have that and still be in a place that awakened incredible passion in so many people? I didn't mean that we could

Adriana Alcântara

help improve the world based on what we did in that office–although that may be open to discussion–but being at *Cartoon* meant that we really had a phenomenal power to have a positive impact. And there we were, drowning in a sea of disorganization, lack of emotional intelligence, not listening to each other, watering down frustrations instead of envisioning our successes. In general, the team focused a lot of energy on personal challenges and frustrations with how the company was dealing with the people involved, so the work itself was not prioritized. With the leadership in the United States, the Brazilian office had no filters for complaints and for the way everyone expressed their opinions. It snowballed: wrong attitudes ended up being normalized eventually generating even worse attitudes.

To start adjusting things, it was really necessary to change some parts that were no longer working, giving a new scope to the new structure. For these vacancies, I brought in two incredible people: Renata Gasperoni for marketing, and Marina Filipe (my former FAAP student, from the class of 2006), for original productions.

Marina studied in one of my first classes at FAAP, when I wasn't very well known as a teacher. I arrived to teach and the students stayed in the hallway. When I saw that no one was coming into the classroom, I went to ask, and they told me that they were waiting for the teacher. Embarrassed, I had to tell them that I was the teacher. They thought I was a night student who had been placed on leave. Yep...

In that class, Marina stood out for her passion for content, especially for children. She loved the segment. She had already worked on the successful kid TV show *Cocoricó* on *Cultura TV* and would be the ideal person for that challenge. As for marketing, the universe enlightened me. I was in the office in the middle of a long weekend holiday and there was almost no one there except Julia Sellare, who had been my editing producer at *Food Network*. I mentioned my desperation, and she said she had an incredible person to recommend: Renata Gasperoni. And, in fact, Julinha was right! Just adding those two to the team had already taken us to another level.

Experienced professionals who had a direct positive impact on the environment and also on other areas. Whether we like it or not, for marketing and original productions to operate well, other areas need to be ready to help.

Connections

Marketing needs the promotional material that is created by the creative team. Production needs marketing to have visibility. Programming needs the dubbing department. Each person functions as part of the gears of a large system. To do this, everyone needs to work on the same team, listening to each other–before, it seemed like we didn't even play the same sport. Before, one group was playing tennis while the other was playing paddle ball, each one playing their own game and with their own individual strategy.

Renata and Marina arrived with the focus of delivering work. They were not part of the network's past. Their past came from outside. What happened in the internal team was what usually happens when someone new arrives. That strange feeling among those who were already on the team and they start to map out the seniority, profile, history of that person, and how they will fit into the group. It is very similar to a new student entering a school. At first, the tendency is for people to try to show their best, until they understand where they are stepping into.

Suddenly, everyone started dancing to the same tune, even developing a genuine interest in each other's work. It was fascinating to observe this evolution! From this interest in the scope of another area, everyone started to develop much more, as they were exposed to other experiences and ways of thinking, and the same was true for me. The amount of learning I enjoyed from having such a large indirect team with completely different profiles and backgrounds was an incredible opportunity. To have everyone on the same page, it was necessary to understand where each of those people came from. What were the challenges–professional or personal–that they had faced there? What was the reference, or lack thereof, that they had of the market outside of *Cartoon*? This was a very interesting process as each person on that team had a different timing to develop a relationship with me. And the key was to listen to each of them!

At first, the only person who bought Adriana Alcântara right away was Patrícia Camargos. She was responsible for the scheduled programming. Yes, the same one I had warned Pablo about not being my thing. The job of analyzing the audience, controlling numbers and changing the strategy to defend against the competition was never my thing. But, as lucky as I am, Pati was a beast. I saw right away that this woman was a jet because she had excellence and unparalleled knowledge in what she did.

Unfortunately, she was an invisible jet, the kind that not even the sharpest radar could detect because of her very shy profile. She wasn't the kind of person who showed everyone her work, but when she did it, it was almost in hiding. No one saw her, and I thought that was absurd. The worst part was that it made her do more and hide more. We immediately started working to change that.

I started triangulating with her. People would come to me and ask me something related to her area, and I would tell them that the final decision wasn't mine. Yes, an attitude that was so important to me in the past was important to someone else in the future.

"Whatever Pati recommends is what we're going to do because she's the programming expert."

And that was really the truth! Sometimes she would come to me and tell me about a challenge, and I would ask her what she would do. Pati would immediately have two suggestions and recommend the one she thought was the best, and I would just say: "Then that's the one we're going to implement."

Every opportunity I saw to put her on the spot in front of others, I would take advantage of it. It was very gratifying to see that little by little my intervention became unnecessary because she managed herself by building self-confidence in her voice. She was the expert on the subject, and she should be heard and recognized.

There were also situations of connection and listening that were a little more complex, like with Vivian Arias. Vivi was from the creative department, and she was someone who was a little wary of my arrival, or at least that's how I felt. I found out much later that Pablo hadn't been clear with the team that my scope was a little broader than my predecessor's, so the team would ask themselves: "But why is she meddling in this if it's not production or programming?"

Little by little, we started to adjust. Starting with small conversations, I showed my vulnerabilities along with my genuine intention to add value and form a single team. I was transparent even when I didn't agree with the company's stance and, unlike what I did at *Nickelodeon*, I managed to position myself correctly. By talking and listening, I continued to build my reputation in a positive way within the company. I was able to

Connections

see the challenges of each member of the team and be empathetic to their expectations. On some hard work days, it was the few coffees we took while exchanging experiences that brought us closer together. When we got on the same page, she became one of my main allies. Vivi had incredible ideas, very connected to the brand, but every crazy idea she came up with had to be sold internally to the boss, Pablo Zuccarino. "Ready to discuss with Pablo?" She always asked me when we finalized an idea that we thought was amazing.

It wasn't easy. The *Campanha do Agasalho* itself, which I've already mentioned here, had to go through a battle with our boss before it was proposed to the São Paulo government– to the point that *Turner*'s CEO in Brazil at the time, Antônio Barreto, said that if Pablo didn't approve the payment, he would approve it as *Turner*, and that if corporate didn't pay, he would use his own money. Pablo hadn't liked the idea of the drive when we first presented it, because he didn't think it would be good for *Cartoon Network*. I asked Barreto for support. Here's an example of the matrix and horizontal structures: Barreto was the local CEO and understood the strength of the project and its relevance. For Pablo, an Argentine leader who was based in Atlanta and somewhat distant from Brazil, it was difficult to understand.

But there were so many wonderful ideas that were worth defending. Over time, Vivi and I created our own dynamic for how to substantiate our arguments in meetings. She had all the knowledge of the brand, her genius, all of *Cartoon'*s history and all the creative defense, so she was able to put together an argument for why a given project was important. When a question came up, I would respond, explaining how the project in question fulfilled a certain role from a business standpoint. Another question came up, and she would respond with other information, and so we continued.

Of course, sometimes we got hit too, to the point where we had to agree and bow our heads. But that was only for a short time because then we would go back to the work table to preparing for the next round. We would take a speech from Pablo and think about how to rebut his argument, we would redesign everything, practice our pitch, and start a new call, until there was no room for a counterargument, leaving him with only one way to reject our ideas: by simply saying "no", without much basis for doing so.

Vivi and I became an unbeatable duo, and that's how we were able to get incredible projects off the ground. The best example was taking *Cartoon Network* live for the first time with the *Toon-Tubers League*, a project created by Vivi before I joined. *ToonTubers* was born in 2016 in the creative department of *Cartoon Network* Brazil, which chose Rigby and Mordecai, characters from *Apenas Um Show (Just a Regular Show)*, as the channel's official gamers and YouTubers. Even though it was designed for digital, the program quickly reached the Top 10 in audience ratings, which justified taking the next step. However, the step we took was to take *Cartoon Network* live for the first time with an e-league, a kind of video game championship played by influencers.

This project was ambitious in several areas. First, in the technical sense. *Cartoon Network* had never gone live in all its years of existence, and the format requires technical experience that is not found everywhere. However, as I like to say, I am always very lucky and surrounded by incredible people who teach me and motivate me. A few meters away from me sat Fabio Mena, better known as Mena–a "young man" because his trademark is to call everyone young in the most beloved way in the world. As an engineering leader and with years of experience in several places, including the wonderful *TV Globo*, he said: "Young lady, yes, it is possible."

With this answer, which was everything we wanted to hear, we brought Mena into our gang. Within a few hours, the entire *Cartoon* team was thrilled. All that was left was to convince Pablo, and Vivi and I already knew how to solve that.

We weren't afraid and there was nothing we couldn't make happen. This brought an empowerment that spread to everyone. We showed that it was always possible to find a solution for something– whether it was a crazy idea for the channel or a personal problem.

Connections

Our adventures
Vivi Arias

When Adriana arrived to take over as head of *Cartoon Network* in Brazil, I felt a mix of expectations and fears. Part of me knew that our team needed a complete shake-up, and I was glad that this shock would come from such an experienced woman. For those who know the organizational charts of media and content companies, it is no surprise that the leadership is highly masculinized (not to mention ridiculously sexist). My more feminist half was very happy.

The problem was the other half...The one that was still in the process of deconstruction (not to mention highly self-sabotaging), who grew up hearing that "you can't trust another woman". To make matters worse, this half was in the process of healing after somewhat negative situations with other women who were still in the process of deconstruction as well.

So, when Adriana arrived at *Cartoon*, I had two very different wolves acting inside me.

The first was an eager wolf who felt she was ready to take on an even bigger leadership role. I was serving with excellence as the creative manager for the most successful projects for the brand and acting as the interim creative manager for Argentina. On top of that, my show, *ToonTubers*, was doing really well, and we were in the process of approving a somewhat crazy idea: to bring *Cartoon Network* to do a livestream for the first time ever with a gaming league: *ToonTubers League*.

It's funny how our ego prevents us from welcoming new experiences with open arms. I was so focused on myself, my abilities, and my productivity, that I almost missed the chance to learn from someone extraordinarily capable.

But Adriana has a unique way of leading, which is sorely lacking in today's times, and she does it with humanity and common sense.

That's when the other wolf inside of me came on stage, the curious one who can't find a good door open without going in to see what's inside. Maybe I even walked towards that door because of the famous "if you can't beat her, join her," but in accepting the invitation to peek through that little crack that Adriana opened for me, I started to listen to her pain more closely. And isn't it true that everything that woman said made perfect sense?

Little by little, I let my guard down and let Adriana's voice enter, and the sound of it was very welcoming.

I clearly remember a tense meeting when the loudest voices seemed to want to dominate the conversation and completely ignore what I was trying to explain. I was there, in the middle of the arena, defending a crucial point of the *ToonTubers League* alone, and many colleagues and leaders remained silent. In the end, no one wanted to make a decision, and everything was falling on the lap of the smallest fish in the room: me. If the project failed, I would go down in history as the person who took *Cartoon Network* off the air for the first time. And that was a very different story from the one I was trying to write. I learned in a screenwriting class that "action shows character", and it was on that day that I got to know Adriana's personality.

In opposition to all the people that just throw words around, she actually held my hand and put her name tag on the table: "If something goes wrong, we'll make this mistake together."

As time went by, our connection only grew. The countless hours of working together that followed, planning, and structuring projects, not only created a work-life connection that continues to this day–now in another company and with different challenges, and just as enriching–but also made me realize that I had an ally and, ultimately, a mentor by my side. Adriana not only defended her ideas with passion, but also knew how to listen and integrate the views of others into her strategies. Good leadership must be able to bring out the best in people, and Adriana has this skill in abundance.

True growth begins where our certainties end. And at that time, when I first started working with Adriana, I was just scratching the surface of what I could be. By letting my guard down and trusting another woman, I not only learned that she would be there to protect me, but I also learned that she could show me the way so that I could one day possibly protect other women too.

Connections

Vivi Arias is a creative strategist and scriptwriter with over twenty years of experience in the content creation and entertainment industry, fourteen of which she worked in content development, scriptwriting, creative production, and creative strategy for *Warner Bros. Discovery* channels and brands (linear/traditional media and social media), and later, as head of creation at *Cartoon Network* Latin America. She has conducted analysis and development reports for *Particular Crowd*, covering all *Warner Media* general entertainment channels, including *HBO Max*. She currently works as senior creative manager at *Audible* Brazil, responsible for all strategy and scripts for title launch campaigns. Throughout her creative career with the shows she created, she has gathered over 50 million viewers on pay TV in Latin America, and over 1.4 billion views on *YouTube*, in addition to eight nominations and five international awards.

There was also Caroline Andrade, a girl with enormous potential, professionally incredible, but at the same time lacked emotional intelligence which controlled her. Instead of filtering her discontent, she would vent on the "hallway radio" and cause trouble at all levels. If I had a meeting with HR about any subject, I knew that when it was over, I would receive an email or someone would come to me personally to tell me about Caroline, better known as Carolzinha, saying that she had caused a mess, that she had not behaved professionally or that she had said too much. I felt that pain on me, because I felt obligated to help. Her attitude, with a lot of emotion, focused on saying what was wrong and not giving in, reminded me in a way of a younger Adriana. Similar to the case of *Nickelodeon*, when I lost a job that I thought I liked because I didn't know how to control my emotional intelligence or rather because I lacked it. Things were moving forward and the dynamics remained the same until, at a certain point, there was a change in the direct management of her area, and the new leader said the following to Carol:

Adriana Alcântara

"Carol, I heard from HR that you do your job very well, but also that you are a troublemaker. And I want to tell you that there is no room for troublemakers on my team."

Shortly after, she came to my desk with tears in her eyes. I had already gained the trust and built a strong partnership with most of the team as the leader, older, more experienced, and a good listener. She came to me telling me what had happened and holding back all that emotion in the form of a waterfall of tears.

"Grab your badge," I said, as I stood up. "Let's go eat some chocolate cake outside the office."

We went down to a café that was right in front of *Cartoon*, and when we sat down, she burst into tears. I listened to her and said: "Carol, you have a very easy problem to solve because your enemy is yourself, so everything depends 100% on you."

Instead of mentioning the mistakes she was making, I pointed out how she was in control of the situation and would never have to hear from anyone else what she heard, as long as she focused on her work and knew how to control her mouth. Everyone there knew how good she was at what she did. I had already recognized that so had HR. But there was this other side of her that could ruin everything. As I spoke to her, I remembered how I used to think and speak without filters, fighting for what I believed in without limits. My story at *Nickelodeon* was an example of this, but the years of maturity had contributed to an evolution, even if small, so I was able to help someone with knowledge of the subject.

"Make a deal with yourself that instead of speaking a million words per minute, you will speak a hundred per hour. That is your quota. Know when to use it. Ask yourself if you really need to say it. If it will promote an improvement. If not, don't say it."

This strategy forced her to think before speaking because she would need to calculate whether she should "spend" words on that topic or not. It was a technique I used on myself to improve my impulsiveness in caring for all causes for all people.

The strangest thing is that she wasn't even part of my work structure because she was in data and market intelligence. But we got to this point, and for some reason–I bet it was my ability to listen–she came to me. Today she's still on the team, having been promoted a few times. The company has gone through dozens of restructurings and layoffs, but it keeps growing. She channeled all her energy into being better and better. I'm immensely proud of this girl, and I continue to follow her journey hoping that she never needs a piece of chocolate cake again.

The other side of that piece of chocolate cake
Caroline Andrade

I, who love all the variations that chocolate can have, would have never imagined that a piece of cake on a random Wednesday in October 2018 would have such a big impact on my life. I would like to begin my side of the story by mentioning something that I believe is the basis of all this learning: the **power of opportunity** and everything it is capable of changing in someone's life. If someone had told me six years ago everything that I would go through, I would not have believed them. But I do not dare, not for a second, to change a single day of this process.

Starting from the beginning of the story, I want to say that this giant named Adriana has my eternal affection, admiration and gratitude. She was the first of many women I have met in the professional environment to lend me a hand, especially when I most needed help, guidance, a sensitive, generous, and empathetic vision from someone who not only looked at me, but who saw much more than what I was able to see on my own. So, first of all, **thank you very much, Dri!**

I started working at this company when I was very young, at age twenty, and I can safely say that I knew nothing about it! To make things even more complicated, I always had managers who did not give me the proper support, nothing more than just my deliverables and obligations. I spent years without having anyone who looked at me the way any inexperienced young person needs to. I started as an intern until I finished and added some experience at an advertising agency. After all, I had studied advertising and marketing. Unfortunately, this experience was not exactly what I had hoped for. So, at the first opportunity (eight months later), I was approached about a position that would be open for the same area that I had left months before, and I went through the process with the managers. Thus, I returned to the same company where I am today, nine years later– eleven if we count my internship period.

I just didn't know that, at the beginning of 2018, such an intelligent, visionary, experienced, creative, and humane person would contribute so much to my growth, even though she wasn't my manager or even working in the same area as me, but rather, as my main stakeholder in the company. And that's how our paths crossed.

After months of much exchange, lessons, and trust, a new management team came to the area I worked in, which had spent many months without leadership for various reasons. This management team's main objective was to unite the crew which had spent years working practically within the stakeholders themselves. A support area such as data and insights was always there for the others, with no regard for itself as a unit. This management team came to change that, and it did.

At that time, at the age of 25, I had already graduated from college and grad school. I had always been very dedicated to my formal education, but I did not have enough chances to invest in my personal development. I was always very concerned about the technical quality of my work and wanted to be a reference in what I did. In a way, I succeeded, but there was something much more important that I had to learn the hard way. I have received some feedback since then in which I often felt the weight of my personality in the main criticisms of my behavior.

I have to confess that it was extremely difficult over the years to not take this type of feedback personally. Me, who have always been an extroverted person, who talks to everyone (and a lot), and who doesn't feel much discomfort with new or different things, found myself increasingly moving away from my personality to fit into a concept that wasn't necessarily the most correct but was needed to adopt in the corporate world. And I can say that only very recently did I understand that I don't need to give up being who I am to belong on a team.

I learned not to take criticism personally, to read the room I am in, to understand where it is okay to be who I am, to be spontaneous, and to

Connections

bring creativity with my daily tasks and new projects. At the end of it all, my personality actually opens doors for me every day, with wisdom and a lot of experience in knowing how to measure where I put effort and energy and what I can (and should) protect myself a little more. The fact is that I am very grateful for the number of opportunities I have had to learn from my mistakes. I am even more grateful for having met fantastic and distinguished women throughout this professional journey, who have taught me and still do it every day how it is necessary to be calm, patient, resilient, actively listen, have a stance, values, and a lot of trust in others. But above all, in what I believe in and who I am. And that is the power of balance.

I truly believe that every day is a new opportunity to be and do better than the day before. If I hadn't had the opportunity to show who I am and what I'm committed to at work every day, I wouldn't have gotten to where I am today, with my extremely dedicated professional career. And more than that, I make sure that the people around me know that they can count on me. No one is alone on the journey called life, much less in the workplace. If everyone could have a little patience and empathy, chocolate cake episodes wouldn't be isolated. We could reach out to many young (or not so young) talents who, with the information overload and references on the internet today, seem to want much more and want it much faster than before.

Today, I am a specialist at the company where I started as an intern. I am 31 years old and very confident in the process. I know that I still have a huge, challenging, and beautiful path ahead of me because I had the opportunity to learn valuable and powerful lessons from strong and inspiring people. But since that chocolate cake that changed everything in my professional life, I have sought to surround myself with incredible people, from the smallest to the biggest influences in this life, and one day, I hope that I can be the chocolate cake for someone else too in the same way that Hurricane Adriana Alcântara passed through my life and taught me so much. I hope that she continues to inspire and guide me in many areas of life for many, many years, just as I hope to be an inspiring figure for someone else too.

Adriana Alcântara

Caroline Andrade is an insights specialist at *Warner Bros. Discovery*. She began her career at the same company in 2011, where she continues to grow. With a bachelor's degree in marketing and advertising from Mackenzie and a postgraduate degree in business intelligence from ESPM, Caroline believes in the power of opportunities and the power of exchanging experiences and connections that enrich us personally and professionally.

Since connections happen in different ways, Guilherme Oller had a different story. He was the head of audio, far from where I worked, as he was more focused on dubbing and original character voices. In other words, he was at the end of the production chain and didn't have much contact with me, but the news that my desk was a mother's heart must have spread through the "radio," and he came to talk about what was worth reading or doing to improve his work. That moment reminded me a lot of my relationship with Roberto Talma. From then on, we started exchanging a lot of tips on books that could serve as study and learning material for both of us. He wanted to take a course, and even though I wasn't his direct boss, I arranged it with HR so that the company would finance it. He joked that I became his mentor from then on, but the truth is that he did the same for me, updating me on all the must-read bibliography that I wanted to read but didn't have time to look for. Gui and I have been friends for years, always exchanging experiences and tips on reading and listening. He was one of the few people who read this book before it was published to give me his insights.

Another very impressive case for me was of a girl who had a very different profile from mine, a little suspicious and almost skittish. Despite being strong in the way I deal with people in the sense of being demanding, I am also very affectionate, but I had the impression that she looked at me and thought: "How annoying is her good mood and her trying so hard to be my friend". From my side, I looked and saw a Great Wall of China between us. While I was building relationships with everyone, she was inaccessible, to the point where I gave up. She did her job very well, overcoming all the

Connections

challenges of a production, but she seemed to have no intention whatsoever of breaking down the barrier that separated us nor letting me try to break it down.

Until one fine day:

"I came to talk to you because I am disappointed with the raise I received," she told me.

I had fought for the raise, defended it with all my heart, but the amount itself had little flexibility. I heard that and remembered some similar situations that I had already dealt with at other companies and my own experience, when I was earlier in my career. Managers end up not providing context, and a lot of things get lost in interpretations.

"Do you have any references for how this situation works in the corporate world?", I asked.

She didn't. I saw myself in that place a lot. Without having parents in the corporate world, I also, when at that stage of life, had no idea how salary dynamics worked. I must have probably felt that way a few times. But now that I knew how everything worked, I felt obligated to contribute.

"Do you have time now, ten minutes? So sit down, let me tell you a story."

What I told her was basically that I understood that when our salary is small–she was just at the beginning of her career–the percentage increase is not what one might imagine and may not seem significant. Even so, she had received a 20% increase, which is a high-performance increase. I told her that the only time I had seen increases above that rate was 30%, which was usually intended to retain employees. In other words, it would be for a very high-performance professional who received an offer from a competitor and, to keep them from leaving, the company would increase the salary by 30%.

"When you got your raise yesterday, you had two choices," I continued. "You could have walked out of here and celebrated yourself, used that 20 percent boost and had a nice drink to celebrate your achievement, or you could have felt let down. You chose the latter."

This was the scenario, I kept explaining, and it wasn't unique to *Turner*; it was just how the corporate world worked. Monetarily it might not make a huge difference, but it was the only way to move forward, and the next 20 percent would be bigger, and so on, until she could achieve enormous visibility and her performance would catch the attention of her competitors, and then she would be in a position to demand 30 percent. That's how the show goes, and how we approach it is our own choice. She got up, said a random "thank you," and left. I had done my part, but once again I regretted the lack of communication.

The next day, she came back to my table, thanking me for the conversation and saying that I had changed her perspective. I was shocked, because I had not expected my experience or empathy to resonate so much with her. Sometimes we have preconceptions that we should not have, but this case brought me a delightful surprise of seeing that I had been wrong in my reading and that she was not so impenetrable after all. There she was, reaching out. I was so glad we had talked.

"Don't let the monetary value ruin your celebration," I concluded.

I could see in her eyes that something had changed. I told her I understood her, and she somehow understood that I could contribute with something. All I did was understand that she didn't know something. And I, who had been in the same career as she had, could contribute with my experience. That was my role, especially because I had been in that same place.

From then on, our relationship changed. She started to come to me frequently looking for ideas to solve any kind of problem, and I helped her in any way I could. The problems of my teams are and will always be my problem too. They do not only belong to each of them individually. Not allowing me to contribute to the fight for the right things is what drives me crazy!

I also learned a lot from her, in many ways. First is that there was no point in me thinking that I would be welcomed by everyone. Even with my friendly demeanor, some people simply don't connect that way. But when you start listening to them, it's possible to find a way to build a good relationship, even with such different profiles and without much initial affinity. And, in fact, these differences can add up. She was in her early twenties, a digitally savvy person, a die-hard fan of *Cartoon Network*, someone who really loved that place. Her knowledge of what the younger generation thought, talked about, and was interested in was very valuable to

Connections

me. In the end, maybe I learned more from her than she learned from me. She stayed at the company and got a few promotions, and I sincerely hope that she celebrated each of these recognitions, regardless of the financial compensation.

And that was how, brick by brick, we created a very strong bond inside *Cartoon*. Things became lighter, and conversations reached a new level. People started to be more open, willing to help each other, develop each other, and contribute to getting everyone to this point. It was something we all built, something very special. There was confidence in everyone's professional ability, and we became very close on a personal level.

    I arrived at *Cartoon* with a certain level of maturity having already been through a lot and having had the opportunity to train myself in the sense of listening, learning how people work, learning how they think and knowing what they need. Over the years, we build up a portfolio of knowledge about types of people, and our sensitivity also improves. And I emphasize that, for my part, I believe that the main role I had was to listen. Understand that it is not *listening*, if the other person's voice enters your ear and you are already thinking about what to respond, but listening with the legitimate intention of understanding the other person, where they are coming from. When you listen to people, you learn.

    But of course, the magical phase had to come to an end. I joke that I managed to get fired from the job where I had, perhaps, performed my best. According to my boss, with the new structure there was no room for a leader of my seniority in Brazil. The company was adjusting its structure to launch *HBO Max* and the leaders would be based in Miami, which was not an option for me.

    I was devastated, feeling wronged, and it seemed like I had the same lump in my throat that I had when I left *Nickelodeon* under extremely different circumstances. I had difficult days when I stopped believing in myself. This is the biggest problem: if we don't believe in our own potential, no one else will, and this will be evident in any job interview. No job loss changes the lessons we have learned along the way, and this should always be remembered. Instead of focusing on those difficult days when I felt like nothing, I prefer to record the recognition I received from those who really mattered when it was time to leave. The entire team put together a Christmas gift box to say goodbye to me.

On Christmas Day, a week after I left, my husband took a bright green box from under the tree and handed it to me, saying that my *Cartoon Network* team had surprised me. I immediately started crying, even before I opened it. Inside this magical box were letters from each member of the team, an album with photos of our history together, and several mementos. This box was worth more than all my time at *Cartoon Network* because it was the materialization of everything I had managed to contribute and the recognition of those who truly cared about me. This box became my source of self-confidence, inspiration, and a kind of lucky charm in every job interview I had from then on. We were at the end of the pandemic, the market was at a standstill, and I was 48 years old not knowing if that would be my last experience in the corporate world.

Listening

Daniela Branco

The journey to build a cohesive and successful team is full of challenges and opportunities for growth. It is a delicate dance between embracing individual differences and channeling these diversities into a common goal.

My professional trajectory was deeply influenced by the inspiring figure of Adriana, whom we affectionately call Drica.

Our connection began in 2004, when I was studying radio and TV at FAAP, in São Paulo. That year, we were going to have a TV Production class and we were surprised by the presence of the youngest professor in the school. At less than thirty years old, she had already completed her master's degree at NYU, worked at the cable TV channel *Nickelodeon* (which was incredible for radio and TV students), and was also a university professor. A figure completely opposite to the traditional old-school professors of the communications school. The truth is that it took us a while to realize that she

Connections

was the professor, and not a new student. And that's how her nickname came along: Wonder Woman.

Since then, Drica has become our personal Wonder Woman: mentor, friend, professional role model and networking queen. She encouraged us in the way any college student would hope: to challenge the institution's processes to produce the best TV show possible. That's how, with the project *Noutras Bandas* (which could be translated to *Bands and Places*) which we still remember today, the connections between classmates emerged, even reflected in Professor Tondella's radio shows, *Gravidade* and *Feira Livre*. The class remained united and our passion for making TV only grew, fighting to use three cameras on the outside, having the biggest set or more time in the editing room.

But the connection didn't stop there. When we met, Drica and I discovered that our families were related. At the time, I was also studying fashion and had an accessories brand. That's when we discovered that Drica had one of my bags, which she had received from her friend Fernanda, who curiously enough, is the ex-wife of my cousin, Jayme Monjardim. In addition, Drica had worked with my cousin Juliana Monjardim on the soap opera *Chiquinha Gonzaga*, when they were both actresses. These connections marked the beginning of the twenty years that followed.

No wonder, Drica was the class's godmother, representing all our dreams for a professional future. She also connected me to my first internship at the production company *MZ Filmes*, bringing together not only me, but also two other *curucos* (a word she affectionately used to call us). From that point on, we began our professional journey together with her always mentoring and guiding me. I was hired at this production company and later worked in dramaturgy at the main television stations in São Paulo. After some time in Barcelona, where I sought to give my career a new direction with a grad study in market trends, behavior, and global consumption, Drica was there to help me get back into the Brazilian market. I went to work in advertising and events agencies, while Drica helped me with connections for the next step. At the same time, she was looking for someone with experience in marketing and TV to join her at *Food Network* Brazil.

Adriana Alcântara

I vividly remember the moment she asked me to join the *Food Network* team. She called me in the middle of the afternoon, and I was at the agency where I worked. We went to lunch the next day, and she said, "Dani, after putting together a puzzle, I spent the last five months looking for someone like you, but I had an old image of you in my head, and I think this challenge is right for you right now."

From that moment on, we began a new chapter, one of the most important in my professional life. Launching the *Food Network* in Brazil was incredible, working with food content was extremely rewarding, and Drica, as my manager, gave me all the autonomy and trust I needed to create innovative projects. But above all, she showed me the path to building a team, hiring people based on their potential, and not being limited by their resumes or degrees. She saw individual potential and believed that, when brought together in a healthy and encouraging environment, personal skills could unfold in surprising ways. She taught me to trust and empower the team by giving them autonomy and recognition. This leadership approach allowed me to achieve my best performance and, consequently, drive the collective success of the team.

Together, we created an incredible group of women, each bringing their own unique strengths and perspectives. Beatriz Gomes (Bea), a brilliant intern, was hired and is now an executive at *Google*. Clara Camargo, a former ballerina and actress who pursued a new career in her thirties, was studying social media when I suggested to Drica for her to join the team—an idea she immediately embraced. And Vittória Caxeiro, who joined the team as an intern, created amazing PowerPoint presentations and later joined Drica at *Cartoon Network*.

In addition, we had Beatriz Cifu and Paula Garcia from the content creation team. Paula also studied at FAAP with me and the connection with Beatriz was so strong that, combined with Drica's sensitivity to put together a compatible team, we became great friends.

I started out as a marketing manager until the day Drica invited me for coffee and handed me a red envelope. Inside was my promotion to director of marketing and partnerships. Another day I will never forget. I looked at her and said, "Are you crazy?" Drica believed in me from the very beginning, long before I believed in myself. Under her management style, I

Connections

achieved my best. I saw how security, trust, and autonomy are essential for quality delivery, all accompanied by recognition.

That was when she reminded me of a phrase she had said to me the other day, while we were in a taxi returning from an interview we gave to the Trade newspaper *Meio & Mensagem*: "You are among the 10% of top performers, believe me." This phrase was so striking that, to this day, my husband repeats it to me.

Since college, she has encouraged us to push the boundaries, think outside the box, and value connections. From the moment I met her, she stood out as an exceptional professional and a natural leader. Her passion for her work, her innovative vision, and her ability to build motivated teams have been fundamental to my professional growth.

When *Discovery* acquired the *Food Network*, we faced a turbulent period of change and uncertainty. When Drica told me about her departure from the *Food Network* to *Cartoon Network*, all I could think about was how I would make the transition without her. Not only because of the work itself but because I would be taking on a crucial leadership and motivational role at a delicate time for the entire team. It was thanks to her and her leadership skills that I embraced this role and determined that we would get through the next few months in a positive way. And not just me, but my entire team would be invited to stay at *Discovery*.

Those were months of great excitement. With the soundtrack of "Dog Days are Over" and Wonder Woman poses, we prepared for our first meeting at *Discovery*. We went there and rocked it, presenting cases that *Discovery*, a giant cable TV network that is much more mature than our *Food Network*, had never achieved. We left such a good impression that the plan worked: everyone was invited to join the *Discovery* team.

However, not everything was a walk in the park. I found myself in a very different environment in terms of culture. People focused on individual goals and a sense of fear of making mistakes– which did not favor my best performance, or perhaps anyone else's. Adding to this challenging scenario, I accepted the mission of leading and uniting three areas under a new structure, composed of completely different people, who needed to change the segmented way of thinking to broaden the scope. Working on individuality and finding the strengths of each person was essential to

Adriana Alcântara

transform the team and choose project leaders regardless of their main area ofactivity.

It was at that moment that, even from a distance, Drica never stopped helping and supporting me. When I shared that I was suffering from burnout and its effects on my entire life and that that culture was not for me, especially after my maternity leave, she did not hesitate to encourage me to find a way out.

So, I embraced the entrepreneurial journey, revamping my family's historic snack bar, and there was Drica, ordering snacks every week and giving me feedback on the fries. It was at that point that our paths crossed again with another link added: Marcia Fernandes. Together, we launched *TriHub*, a branding and content creation consultancy.

A few months later, Drica was invited to lead *Audible*'s operations in Brazil. Soon after, I had the pleasure of joining her once again, in this new and incredible challenge. She needed help even before putting the team together and knew that my maturity at the time was quite holistic, and that I could help in several areas. I was the first to arrive and performed in different positions. Whatever was needed, I threw myself on it and got it done. Drica praised me and I thought: *Wow, I'm getting back to being myself after not believing in my potential for months.*

I firmly believe that there are relationships, both personal and professional, that bring out the best in us. Just as there are relationships that bring our worst. I believe this so much that Gabriel García Márquez's quote opened my wedding website: "I love you not for who you are, but for who I am when I am with you."[12] I am positive that my husband and Adriana are the two people who bring out the best in me.

Our connection and other links that came from her make me wonder if I didn't also work at *Cartoon*, for example. I've heard so many stories and participated, even from afar, in achievements and celebrations. When I hear some of them, I'm sure I already know and/or am close to these people. With this feeling, I remember the day I met Renata Gasperoni, a person I'd heard so much about through members of my team at *Discovery*,

---

[12] "Impactful quotes from Gabriel García Márquez". *Época Negócios Magazine*, April, 17th 2014. Avaiable at:<https://epocanegocios.globo.com/Inspiracao/Vida/noticia/2014/04/frases-marcantes-de-gabriel-garcia-marques.html>. Visited at Sept., 23rd, 2024.

Connections

friends and Drica herself. "Renata, haven't we met before?" I asked. Even Drica thought we knew each other. Once again, the power of connections and Drica's careful choices in team building brought Renata and I together in the same challenge of launching *Audible* in Brazil. The connection was instantaneous, and the work simply flowed.

After working in an environment where relationships were not built and management was based on fear, and I began to question whether I wanted to return to the corporate world, I was able to reflect a lot on the ideal company I would accept to work for. The valueswere reversed: the position and even the salary were no longer at the top of the list, but rather the company culture, the manager, and the work environment began to dictate my next steps.

Today, I am very happy to have chosen *Audible*. I am very happy to be back in the same boat as Drica, uniting lifelong connections from FAAP, *Food Network*, *Cartoon Network*, *Discovery* in a new project that puts people at the center, as the value and soul of the business. A kind culture that has active caring as one of its principles.

To get here, I went through many coaching exercises to list "what I want", "what I don't want", "what is my ideal job" and several discussions about what *flow* is, a state of mental flux that can be used in various aspects of life, such as sports, meditation and work, and how to achieve it. It can be achieved when we balance challenges and skills, that is, when our strengths and values come together to carry out a job. One of the best feelings a professional can have is to enter a state of flow: work flows effortlessly, distractions disappear, and one can even lose track of time. In this state, productivity and creativity soar, allowing us to carry out complex tasks without difficulty.

As I reflect on this journey, I am confident that today I have found my flow. I am immensely grateful for the connections I have built and the collective spirit I have cultivated. The lessons I have learned about the importance of building cohesive teams, valuing individual talents, and fostering an environment of trust and collaboration are precious to me and will stay with me forever. I am certain that these are the main tools that allow us to achieve true and lasting success in the professional world.

Daniela Branco Daniela is the director of *"Amazon marketing"* at *Audible*, responsible for the company's communication across all *Amazon* channels in Brazil and emerging markets. With over eighteen years of extensive experience in the communications and marketing market, the executive previously served as marketing director at *Scripps Networks*, where she was responsible for the launch strategy for the *Food Network* channel. With the acquisition of *Scripps* by *Discovery*, Daniela joined the *Discovery* team, expanding her responsibilities to include promotions and digital strategies. She co-founded the companies *Hamburguinho 1974* and *TriHub Strategic Consulting, Marketing & Content Creation*, and also worked at advertising and event agencies such as *Moma* and *Sistole Brasil*, and at the open TV channels *SBT*, *Band* and *Cultura*. Benjamin's mother, Daniela has a degree in radio and TV from FAAP, with a postgraduate degree in coolhunting: design and global trends from Universitat Pompeu Fabra in Barcelona, in addition to having specialized in visual anthropology at PUC-SP and in product management at ESPM.

Listening

Marina Filipe

They say there is only one way for introverts to make friends: to be adopted by an extrovert. In the professional scene, the logic is similar. Drica is *the* extrovert. I am the introvert who was lucky enough to be "adopted" by her. And with the capacity for observation that introspection gave me, since the first day I saw her, I have watched her and learned as she does what, in my opinion, is her greatest skill: managing people. But let's go back to our first day and leave "people" for other paragraphs.

Connections

Who was that woman that, looking like a girl, had gone unnoticed, at first, among those students who were already skeptical that anything useful could come out of a TV production class at college? I asked myself this question as I watched her. And she told me about her experience. She was basically who I would like to be one day, but I did the math and it seemed impossible to achieve so much in such a short time, since only ten years of life separated her from me. In a short time, the production class had become popular, challenging, and fun. Only now, as I stop to write this text, I realize that Drica did with each one of us in that class the same thing I saw her doing fifteen years later on *Cartoon Network*: she listened to us. And by listening, she gave a chance to that introspective young woman with great ambitions. She listened to me and found a potential that I still struggle to see today. She listened to me and adopted me.

College became a thing of the past, but not the connection. At multiple points in my career, Drica was present: directly, leading some short project in which I was involved. Or as a mentor, always helping me make the best decisions and the best moves. I never participated in a selection process without her being there closely, helping me with the interviews or salary negotiations. The dream of working directly together always existed, but it took more than a decade for it to happen. And it happened when I least expected it.

I was in the middle of a set, watching the rehearsal that preceded a live show. For someone who does what I do, this description is a dream. In my case, at that moment, it was a dream that came true. At the time, I was a sales and format adaptation executive at *BBC Studios* in Brazil. The phone rang and I answered. It was Drica. The day before, I had seen an article in a magazine about her going to *Cartoon Network*. After congratulating her, I heard: "I want you to come work with me, taking care of original productions." I put my head down on the set table and thought, what a perfect timing. I told her that I was doing well, that I was earning well, but then Drica's second greatest skill came into play: persuasion.

She had time, and she used it to convince me little by little. It wasn't that difficult, I had grown up watching *Cartoon Network*, and original productions were a career goal. But, I was afraid of exchanging something wonderful for the unknown. It took me months to accept participating in the selection process. I still joke with Pablo Zuccarino today that he didn't want me. The truth is that his vision made sense. There I was, with no experience in animation, applying for a senior position at *Cartoon Network*. But as I said before, Drica sees the potential in people beneath the first layers. She knew about my dedication, my passion and that, with my experience in production, I had what it took. Drica convinced Pablo.

I found a hostile environment. Drica had just arrived a few months earlier and was still exploring the surroundings. Many people still looked suspicious at her. I was seen as the pupil. I inherited the hostility, but without Drica's ability to deal with the situation. Introspective, I did what introspective people do best: I immersed myself in the work. And from my desk, I observed what was perhaps the most masterful work of people management that I have ever seen.

In just a few months, even amidst eye-rolling, Drica managed to get big projects off the ground that had never been done before. What would have been a simple project became "Jorel's Brother Month," with giant rain boots in São Paulo's subway to collect shoes or a truck full of Sansãos walking around the city, celebrating "Mônica's Month." Sansão and Monica are part of the most famous Brazilian Comics Books crew. All of these actions with original productions as the central focus made me work with absolutely every team at *Cartoon Network*. Over time, most of the hostility subsided, and Drica's desk became the place where everyone knew they could go and be welcomed. Drica always had her door open (just like in college), and the more people were heard and the more projects came to fruition, and the more autonomy I was given.

With an almost blind trust that taught me more than any college degree, I was in charge of the original productions while Drica orchestrated people and ideas. And so, I learned that working with Drica means working as a team. There is no way to escape it. In no way are you going to want to escape it. Those were magical times. Today, six years later, still at *Cartoon Network*, I have to face the fact that the next step in my career requires a skill that is not innate to me. I need to connect, do politics, and manage people. A huge challenge that, once again, leads me to have Drica as a model, as a mentor. The passionate and humane way in which she mobilizes us to use our strengths towards a common goal. The determined way in

Connections

which she takes an idea under her wing and only rests once it is on paper. The way she directs different interests towards a single purpose. I will never do the same. We are not the same. But I am once again certain, I have the best teacher.

Marina Filipe is the Senior Manager of Original Productions for *Warner Bros. Discovery* in Brazil for children's brands, including *Cartoon Network*, *Cartoonito* and *Discovery Kids*. She is responsible for the development and production of original local Brazilian content. Her previous experience includes companies such as *BBC Studios*, as a development producer, and *Endemol Shine Brasil*, as production director. She holds a degree in radio and TV from FAAP, a master's degree in film and television business from FGV and a master's degree in neuroscience, education and child development from PUC-RS.

Adriana Alcântara

Connecting the dots

- We don't need to be right every time, but we need to be heard. This increases the feeling of security in the corporate environment.

- It is important to always be open to hearing different things, because there will certainly be hidden treasures in each speech and path that can help us create and strengthen connections. When you start listening to the other person, it is possible to find a way to build a good relationship, even with different profiles and without much initial affinity.

- It is worth noting that, here, it is not about hearing. When the person's voice enters our ear, we are already thinking about what to respond, but listening with the legitimate intention of understanding the other person and the place where they come from, you learn.

- Knowing how to listen and integrate other people's views into your strategies is something that will set you apart as a leader. Active listening, in addition to being a great ally when it comes to helping bring out the best in people, is also something that positively helps your internal reputation within a company.

SHARE YOUR ANSWERS #CONNECTIONSBOOK

Connections

Now it's your turn!

It's time to strengthen our active listening skills! The following exercise is simple and practical and will help you sharpen this skill. Let's do it?

1. During a short conversation, focus fully on what the other person is saying, without interrupting. Try to avoid letting pre-judgments get in the way. Ideally, do this exercise with someone who is presenting a different point of view than you, so you can practice resisting the trap of already having your standard response ready to disagree.

2. When the other person finishes speaking, summarize what they said in a single sentence to confirm that you understood them correctly. This does not necessarily mean that you have changed your opinion, but verbalizing the other person's point of view helps you internalize it in your thinking and consider changing your position. The important thing is not whether or not you change your position, but that you are genuinely open to listening.

3. Repeat this process as often as you can to improve your active listening!

Adriana Alcântara

CHAPTER 7
Empathy

I find it difficult to talk about diversity without talking about opportunity. I think that a person's potential is the path they take between a starting point and a finishing point. Unfortunately, people don't start from the same starting point. I, for example, started ahead of almost every other runner.

I was born into a family that wanted me very much along with all the conditions necessary to have a child. I never had to worry about whether there would be food on the plate or if we would end up being evicted because we couldn't pay the rent. In the winter, I knew I wouldn't be cold. In the summer, I knew I could travel and have fun without ever thinking about any of those things.

There was no violence in my home. I had access to healthcare and education. I checked the list of so many basic conditions for a person to live up to their potential that, before any starting gun was fired, I was already much closer to the finish line than the starting line. Unfortunately, however, such circumstances do not correspond to the reality of most people.

When I look back on my journey, it is impossible not to ponder the fact that all these advantages come from a place of great privilege. At least, I also believe, I did my best to live up to all the opportunities I had since birth.

My personal sphere also had far fewer obstacles than one would imagine. I got married at 36, while having a very mature and established career, to a wonderful man who loves and respects me. The following year, I fulfilled my dream of becoming a mother with the arrival of my daughter, Maria Victoria, without any challenges in getting pregnant. Quite the opposite, it happened when I changed my pill, when the contraceptive coverage dropped from 99% to 70%. Already pregnant, but still without knowing it, I took two packs of pills thinking that the new medication was making me very sleepy and nauseous as a side effect. Well, with so much information at my disposal, I was pregnant and only found out when I was already eleven weeks.

I also understand that many people are unable to form the family of their dreams, cannot find a life partner, and cannot or do not get pregnant. So, more than a privilege, I have experienced a true blessing.

In terms of race, the same thing. I am white with Italian heritage – I just don't have blue eyes like my siblings, Fernando, Renato, and Elora, who inherited this characteristic from my mother. When I see the challenges faced by other races in maintaining their culture and finding space to stand out, it becomes clear that there is more than just a dynamic of starting point and finishing line. Besides that, we need to add the fact that the distance between one and the other is even wider. White skin color, by itself, not only receives miles of privileges, but black skin is also pushed in the opposite direction.

I don't know how many decades or centuries it will take to make the necessary historical reparations, but I do know that offering more opportunities is now within reach. And believe it or not, even this has its challenges.

In 2004, I did a soap opera on Record called *Turma do gueto* (*Guetto Crew*)–again in a *Casablanca* production, of course–and almost the entire cast was black, very different from what happens in the companies, schools and colleges I've worked at.

Right out of the bet, assembling an experienced cast was already a challenge. Although Brazil has a predominantly black population, when casting, the search had to take place in other agencies and places that were not the most used. Obviously, it would not be difficult to trace within the history of Brazilian soap operas how black characters were a minority and, most of the time, of very little importance to the central plots. For a long time, these were the only opportunities offered to them.

However, the incredible thing is that the soap opera had a very high audience. It aired alongside *Programa da Hebe* at SBT and won in the ratings–something unheard of for Record at that time. An article at the time had the headline *"Turma do gueto* beats the couch crew in audience"– referring to the legendary Hebe Camargo's sofa.[13]

Programs that featured black people and told stories they could relate to were so rare that the soap opera took off and became the channel's flagship. I had a big role in it but was never recognized in the places I went, and I don't think any of my school or work colleagues saw me on the show.

However, it wasn't uncommon for gas station attendants, obviously people who had less educational opportunities, to come running to take pictures and ask for my autograph when I stopped to fill up my car. This was another situation in which I came face to face with the fact that we have a divided world.

Yet another evidence that television drama merely replicated our reality: certain jobs and opportunities were reserved for the black population. Almost all the doors accessible to white people would be difficult for black people to access, with rare exceptions.

Only in recent years–a much longer time than it should have been– has society become more concerned about creating more balanced teams in this regard, and the enormous difficulty in recruiting black people in large companies persists, two decades after what I witnessed in the Record soap opera. This challenge is at the root of many things, as is social inequality itself in Brazil. In my opinion, an important front to change this sad reality is education.

We all know that in the Brazilian corporate job market, the starting point is higher education. Assuming that the person had attended college, the rule would move to: which college? In almost all cases, we end up leaving out many people and giving opportunities to those who have always had them. But of course, to even reach this stage and have access to higher education, this education would need to start in childhood. It is necessary to ensure that the child goes to school and has access to formal and informal education. Formal education is the classroom, that is, a child needs to study. The informal, and even more important one, is to ensure that the child is safe at home, that they understand their rights and have the maximum amount of information to defend themselves. This is a huge challenge, and it is not

---

[13] The *Turma do Gueto* won against the madam's crew. Newspaper *Agora SP*, São Paulo, Supplement Show!, May, 11th 2004.

Connections

going to be possible to bring everyone closer to the starting point overnight. But to reduce the distance between them, it is important that each of us contributes in whatever way we can.

In this scenario, where we seek to reduce inequalities from childhood and ensure more equitable opportunities, protecting children goes beyond access to education. It is also essential to ensure that they grow up in safe environments, both in the physical and digital worlds. It was with this in mind that, after seven years working with children's channels and content, I became very attached to this audience and its universe, and because of this world of connections, I entered into one of the most fulfilling projects I have ever experienced. It all started through my sister Priscila, the daughter from my stepmother Mabel's first marriage. Pri lives in the United States and works in wealth management and treasury. When she moved to the country, after having lived and giving birth to two daughters in Canada, she looked for a social project in which she could participate by doing volunteer work. She found *Protect Us Kids* (*PUK*), a nonprofit dedicated to protecting at-risk youth from cybercrime so they can navigate cyberspace freely without being targeted by people who want to take advantage of them. *PUK* was founded by Veda Woods, the former head of cybersecurity for the *Recovery Accountability and Transparency Council* during President Barack Obama's presidency and a veteran of information security, including stints at *Morgan Stanley* and *Capital One*.

    Veda is one of those people you connect with in seconds, due to her passion and involvement with the *PUK* cause. I immediately admired her and thought about how I could contribute by using my network of contacts and my expertise to bring this project to Brazil, through a campaign that would generate more information about the risks of the Internet and have a media reach that would bring results.

    PUK already had volunteers in the marketing area, but they were far removed from the Brazilian reality. We needed to adapt and guide all the visual arts and messages so that they would work here. Then, we had to ensure that we had the rights to use the image so that the photos and videos could be used outside the United States. Brazil is a highly regulated country, and we only discover the intricacies of the challenges once the plane is in full flight, so the only way is to repair it and refuel it in the air.

Adriana Alcântara

Unlike what happens in other countries, Brazil has protection for commercials to be produced here, thus generating a boost for the creative economy and an opportunity for producers, actors, etc. Since the *PUK* commercial was produced in the United States, the fees to "naturalize" it and use it in Brazil were unaffordable. This took us back to square one, which was, we would have to build the materials to be used in Brazil and nothing that existed abroad could be used. When I say we, in practice it was me, because Veda and Pri were in the United States and I was the only one to lead the cause in Brazil–or at least formally speaking–but it wouldn't be long before my connections came into play to support me in this goal.

With the artwork and messages finalized, I began to develop what would be the script for the TV commercial made in Brazil. With a life built in this universe, I began knocking on the doors of all the contacts I had to make it happen, and it happened through connections I built at different moments in my career and life. Together, we created a beautiful campaign which had several collaborators.

Ludmila Pimenta, a partner at the production company *Casa de Vídeo*, helped us put together the TV ad. Lud joined my team when I was at *Nickelodeon*. She arrived to do the external recordings for the shows, which is the material that shows recorded in a studio usually have to take a breather. Very sweet and super competent, Lud earned her place on the team and also became friends with me and Luísa Fernandes. After that first time, we worked together when I was at *OiTV* and Ludmila was already at *Casa de Vídeo*. After a few years at the production company, she became a partner and, as such, was able to help us with the production of the Brazilian commercial.

To avoid spending even more on a voiceover, we used my rusty acting skills, and I recorded it myself. To do this, I used my dear *Casablanca*, which I practically consider myself an emotional partner, just not included in the contracts, tax ID, and other paperwork. Whenever I need something, Patrick Siaretta, Arlette's son, solves it and makes everything happen. This friend is always by my side, supporting me, encouraging me at any moment, and believing in me when I start to doubt my ability to make things happen.

For the static art, we needed a printing company, and my school friend Rodrigo Abreu also made the strength of the Alpha-Graphics printing

Connections

company available for the cause. Abreu, as he has always been and is called by his friends, was in my class at Pueri Domus. We grew up together, and our sports teams proudly wore the green Abreu stationery t-shirts. All the other classes looked at Class B with a certain jealousy, since we were the only "sponsored" class. Always generous and kind, Abreu is that friend who is always ready to help. We are still friends to this day and, of course, he offered to help us with the PUK cause, printing everything that was needed.

We were still missing a way to showcase the work. Years before, I had already done a great subway campaign with the *Food Network* and I called Juliana Alcides to propose an exhibition of awareness tips for young people, children and their parents, and Juliana agreed right away. You know that person who embraces social causes without an inch of hesitation? Well, you've noticed how lucky I am to have friends like that.

The exhibition was covered by the press, by several TV channels, and print media making the message reach far beyond the millions of people who use the yellow and purple lines of the São Paulo subway. We used the TV spot inside the subway cars, which have screens on board and are a great vehicle for this type of content.

The result made me proud and more confident to do something even better. In the second campaign, I got support from *Grupo Globo* and its cable channel aimed at children, *Gloob*. This only happened thanks to my friend from *Globosat*, Tatiana Costa, who not only opened the door for me, but slammed it wide open. So much so that the project ended up going to *Globo* corporate, and we got space on all *Grupo Globo* channels. In addition, *Gloob* thought it would be really cool to have a TV spot with a message aimed at children, after all, the commercial we produced spoke to adults, parents, and guardians, and not directly to them. To my surprise, the channel put together a film with animations, raising awareness among children about internet safety. I had never imagined that *Gloob* would give us this gift, because I know very well how much work this requires and how much work TV professionals have to do on a daily basis. In an ideal world, teams would be much larger, but they're not. So, everyone has to multiply themselves– that's why I know it was really hard to accommodate that extra spot.

To grow even more, Pedrão, Pedro Barbastefano Jr., from *29 horas*, a magazine that is available free of charge at airports and on airplanes, joined the project. The company is also responsible for electronic media at *Congonhas* Airport in São Paulo and *Santos Dumont* Airport in Rio de Janeiro. I had met him at the Food Network, when he opened a very important space to promote the show *Um dia de chef* (*A Day as a Chef*), with Emmanuel Bassoleil. A personal friend of Emmanuel, he supported his show when he was starting his career on TV with us and became an important connection.

Pedrão welcomed us with open arms and we placed our films in the media displays at the airports of São Paulo and Rio de Janeiro, and as a bonus, we received a beautiful article in the magazine *29 horas*. When I thought the campaign was over, I received a call from the social communications department of the Salvador subway in Bahia. They had seen the campaign through the news coverage we had in São Paulo and asked for my contact information for Juliana Alcides. Two weeks later, our exhibition was in the subway of the capital of Bahia, where it remained for two months.

Seeking safety and education for children and young people, especially in vulnerable situations, is *PUK*'s main goal. I believe that this work was already a start, even though it is a grain of salt compared to what needs to be done. These campaigns follow a kind of snowball logic. The more things you achieve the greater the chance you have of achieving even more. When the campaign is small or when we are looking for a first partner, nothing moves forward. It seems that people do not trust projects on paper. When you show that you already have a partner on board, the second one comes quickly, the third even faster, and before you know it, the thing has become huge and there is a lot of good energy returning to each of the participants, to whom I owe my eternal gratitude.

The Internet is a powerful way that can help in education, but it can also pose many risks. If we minimize the risks by providing information and awareness, it can help in the education and development of many people and contribute to reducing the distance between people's starting points. I am not a dreamer, and I know it is just a drop in the ocean, but if each of us does a little to reduce the distance between these starting points, perhaps they will be less discrepant for future generations. Without a doubt, we need much more than that, large-scale structural projects, housing–which is my sister's

Connections

Duda Alcântara focus, which I recommend connecting and getting to know her on LinkedIn.

Aiming to increase my contribution through *Protect Us Kids*, in early 2024, three incredible women contacted me, interested in PUK. First, Juliana Alcides, who had left *ViaQuatro* and had already been a partner in my projects, but on the other side of the table. In addition to her, a former FAAP student contacted me through LinkedIn: Marília Santos. After college, she followed a career similar to mine, mostly in cable TV channels. Having become a mother, she was looking for an organization that would contribute to the better use of technology for children.

To complete our fantastic four, Clarissa de Oliveira, who is living in New York, had previously come into contact with the PUK campaign when she worked at Gloob. Through a mutual friend and former colleague at *Globosat*, Claudia Lira, she approached me to contribute to the project. Thus, we began our next PUK campaign in Brazil, hoping that it will be infinitely bigger in 2024 and in the coming years, and that it will help with information, education and opportunities.

Who knows, maybe little by little, we can make a difference on this immense ocean. If you are interested in the cause, connect with us on LinkedIn. It will be our pleasure!

Empathy

Veda Woods

Being an introverted empath has always colored my experiences, both personally and professionally. This aspect of my identity has been a guiding light, a source of strength, yet also a challenge to navigate in a world that often misunderstands quiet reflection for weakness and deep empathy for vulnerability.

My introversion and empathy have shaped me into a natural nurturer, someone who values deep, meaningful connections above all. Relationship building isn't just a part of my career strategy. It's a core part of who I am. I've found that creating these connections requires not just understanding others but also a deep understanding of oneself. This introspection has allowed me to recognize my own strengths and limitations, enabling me to offer genuine support and understanding to those around me.

In the early days of my career, the challenges were palpable. The workplace often seemed designed for the extroverted, where loud voices often drowned out the quiet. But I learned to see my introverted empathy not as a hindrance but as a unique tool. It allowed me to listen deeply, to understand the unspoken emotions of my colleagues and leaders, and to build relationships on a foundation of genuine understanding and trust.

This approach to relationship building became my signature, my way of turning perceived weaknesses into undeniable strengths. As I climbed the professional ladder, I found that my ability to nurture relationships, to empathize deeply, even from a place of quiet observation, was what set me apart. It enabled me to lead with compassion, to foster a culture of inclusivity and understanding, and to inspire those around me to embrace their authentic selves.

My journey has taught me the power of balance—balancing my introverted nature with the demands of leadership, and balancing my empathy with the need for self-care. It's a delicate dance, one that requires constant attention and adjustment, but it's also incredibly rewarding. My introversion and empathy have allowed me to create meaningful, lasting relationships, both in my personal life and in my professional endeavors.

As I look to the future, I see a world where the quiet strength of introverted empaths is recognized and celebrated, where the power of deep, empathetic connection is seen as the cornerstone of successful leadership. My story, woven from the threads of introspection, empathy, and nurturing, is a testament to the quiet power that lies in all of us, waiting to be acknowledged and embraced.

Connections

Veda T. Woods, with over 28 years in the field, Woods is a dynamic force in cybersecurity, recognized for her advocacy and strategic leadership. As the head of the *Global Cyber Security Advisory Group* (GCSA), she blends cybersecurity with sustainability, driving global access to digital protection. Her commitment to digital inclusion has catalyzed initiatives that extend cybersecurity to underserved areas globally. Woods' strategic vision is also evident in her founding of the *Protect Us Kids Foundation*, which directs *GCSA* proceeds to combat the online exploitation of children. A respected voice from Morgan Stanley to the U.S. White House, her work is defined by integrity and a drive to empower through education in cybersecurity sustainability, technology, digital literacy, data privacy, and ethical computing practices.

Adriana Alcântara

Connecting the dots

- Creating connections requires not only understanding others, but also a deep understanding of oneself. This introspection allows us to recognize our own strengths and weaknesses, and opens up the space for us to offer genuine support and understanding to those around us.

- We must always keep in mind that not everyone has the same ease or the same view of things, and that sometimes the content of your message can be compromised by the way you present it. Empathy is a fundamental ally when we need to adjust relationships and have difficult conversations.

- In the end, there is no magic formula for creating these connections that help us climb the corporate ladder, but some ingredients help a lot on this journey. Transparency, synergy and empathy always yield good results, as do luck, trust, courage, flexibility, emotional intelligence and listening.

SHARE YOUR ANSWERS #CONNECTIONSBOOK

Connections

Now it's your turn!

It's time for us to strengthen our empathic capacity. The following exercise, when practiced regularly, will help you better understand the emotions and motivations of others.

1. Think about a recent situation in which you had a disagreement with someone or witnessed an argument.

2. Put yourself in the person's shoes and try to understand how they felt. Ask yourself:

    - "What were they thinking?"
    - "What were their concerns or fears?"
    - "How would I react if I was in the same situation?"

3. Describe below what you think the person was feeling and what may have motivated their actions.

4. How can you connect with this person's challenge and try to help them in some way?

Adriana Alcântara

EPILOGUE

About the connection we created here

I have always dreamed of putting my experiences on paper, hoping to eventually encourage other women to follow the path of leadership and to grow stronger through connections. This book partially existed for a few years, not counting the time it lived only in my head, as a simple desire. When I joined *Audible*, I felt a jolt almost like an external force, encouraging me to make this dream come true. After a few possibilities, I met Anderson Cavalcante who gave me this chance.

Writing it in 2024, when I turned fifty, was a true gift. I think that every year we stop on our birthday to evaluate the previous cycle and plan the next one, but this age is a milestone that makes this reflection even deeper. Putting on paper my experiences, my mistakes, my successes, and above all, the connections I have built, was truly magical.

I wasn't going to celebrate my birthday until I told my friend and sister Mariana Santoro Batochio about it and she organized a surprise party with dear friends. Mari and I have a life of deep connection that resulted in that unforgettable night for me.

A shoulder to always cry on

Mariana Santoro Batochio

We went to the same school the year Dri went to live in Baghdad. Years later (a day I remember as if it was yesterday), I was with my family in a hotel in

Connections

Campos do Jordão (countryside of São Paulo) and I saw the girl who had gone to live in Baghdad walking in my direction. I looked at her and said: "Didn't you live in Baghdad? We went to high school together."

It was on that day that we really connected and that I gained a sister in my heart. There were thousands of trips, stories, laughter, *Frumelo* candies, parties, tears, and moments that I cherish dearly.

Dri has always been that friend who made me proud. She started working early. While we went to parties, she would record the *Walking Show*. I went to so many plays and gave her a standing ovation in the front row. We shared so many achievements and cried so many tears together. Dri has always been an example to me, not only as the perfect friend, but as an impeccable professional, an exemplary daughter, and my best travel companion in the world.

Just like her and most women, I also fought for a place in a predominantly male universe within the realm of auctions. I am part of the second generation of an auction organization and I have witnessed this male world since I was a girl. It is not easy to stand out as a woman in the job market, and since I was never willing to give up my delicacy and at the same time wanted to show that strength often lies in subtlety itself, my sister and I decided to take a stand and created *As Leiloeiras* (The Auction Girls). We brought to this world the feminine and light way of conducting an auction. It was all or nothing, but one thing we were not willing to trade was our light and sweet way. So, step by step, we grew and opened a work front, this time much more connected to the female environment. I know that we are just starting, but I already feel fulfilled to see that the fruits continue to appear and that we continue to have ideas, reinvent ourselves, and have fun. In addition to being the creator of *As Leiloeiras*, I am also a mother. I have three children: Gabriela is 21, Eduardo is 19 and Carolina is 17. And I can say that I leave my example to my daughters, just as my mother taught me: let us always be strong. For me, that is already worth a lot.

Dri and I have never worked together, but I can say that we have worked together on everything, actually. Every step, every challenge, every day of fear or sadness always becomes easier when we share and when we have a true friend to advise us. In the midst of our busy lives, we don't get to see each other as much as I would like, but we know the strength of our friendship. And here I am, once again, dying of pride for this special friend of mine. Congratulations on taking the initiative to tell your successful story. You are a woman who inspires many people. And I am one of them.

> **Mariana Sodré Santoro Batochio** has a bachelor's in advertising and marketing and a bachelor's in law. She has worked for almost three decades at *Sodré Santoro Leilões*, her family's auction organization. She has held several auctions, including charity ones, such as the auction in support of UNICEF, in partnership with *Maurício de Sousa Produções*, auctioning 33 rabbits, of the character Sansão, dressed in clothes designed by Brazilian designers, and also auctions in support of the *Barretos Cancer Hospital*, the *Childhood Brazil Foundation*, the *Protea Institute* and many others.

Well, Mariana made me emotional with my surprise party. There, I saw people who had been part of my story since preschool, like my friend Daniela Turella, who I met when I was three years old. People I had met in my professional life, like Renata Gasperoni, Marina Filipe and Daniela Branco (who also contributed to this book). Friends from college, elementary school, and travels. Watching that group singing happy birthday– yes, that moment when you die of shame–warmed my heart. I had the confirmation that I managed to build strong, lasting, genuine bonds and connections, and that in some way, I was also important to those, who left their families on a Wednesday night to honor me. We are the same human beings, whether we work together or not, and the way we form and value bonds says a lot about who we are.

Professionally, I have undoubtedly been very lucky and have expanded many possibilities. I have had important learning experiences that either came easily or with great difficulty, but in one way or another, they have led me to the next step. Some learnings are still only in theory, but there

Connections

is always time to put them into practice. Along these paths, I have helped and positively influenced people, and I have been guided and influenced by many others, to whom I continue to be grateful and attentive, observing them to learn even more.

Even at fifty, I feel like I still have a lot to do and learn. The world is constantly changing, and learning never ends. Fortunately, with it comes more opportunities for connections. Nowadays, through the digital world, we have an immense ease in connecting and maintaining them, generating projects that can contribute greatly to a better world. Therefore, I want to end this book by extending an invitation: to you, who are reading this, what are your stories? When did you get things right? And how did you learn and rethink when you made mistakes? I would love to hear from you, and it would be a pleasure to connect with you and hear your story. My LinkedIn is waiting for yours. Contact me, so we can exchange experiences:

linkedin.com/in/adrianaalcantara/

I'm looking forward to hearing from you. Thank you for reading and for being another chapter in my journey.

About the Author

Adriana Alcântara has served as the General Manager of *Audible* Brazil since May 2022, where she has spearheaded the company's commercial strategy, launch operations, and service structuring in the region. With a standout career in the content and media industry, she has held leadership roles in business development, production, marketing, and branding across Brazil and Latin America. Her impressive portfolio includes positions at renowned companies such as *Warner Bros., Discovery, Apple, OiTV, Grupo Globo, Viacom Networks Brasil*, and *MSNBC* in New York. The author began her career in the entertainment industry at *Casablanca*, a production company from Brazil.

  Alcântara holds a Master's in Arts and Sciences from NYU and spent over 14 years as a postgraduate professor in business, content, and marketing at FAAP in São Paulo, Brazil. Her diverse background includes working as a TV host and actress in Brazilian theater and soap operas. She co-authors *Rise and Raise Others* (WeBook Publishing, 2024).

www.ingramcontent.com/pod-product-compliance
Lightning Source LLC
Chambersburg PA
CBHW020245010526
44107CB00002B/100